Kill the Chocolate Biscuit

"KILL THE CHOCOLATE BISCUIT"

or Behind the Screen by
Desmond Wilcox and Esther Rantzen

cartoons by Rod Jordan

*From a Godfather !
to a Godmother, & with
love from both of us to
both of you !
Desmond & Esther
xxt*

Pan Original
Pan Books London and Sydney

First published 1981 by Pan Books Ltd,
Cavaye Place, London SW10 9PG

© Desmond Wilcox and Esther Rantzen 1981
cartoons © Rod Jordan 1981
Filmset by Northumberland Press Ltd,
Gateshead, Tyne and Wear
and printed by Richard Clay (The Chaucer Press) Ltd,
Bungay, Suffolk

This book is affectionately dedicated to the memory of John Lloyd, who not only invented the title but discovered the only way to view the world of television – and stay sane.

Acknowledgements

We would like to acknowledge the loyal support of Jenny Hearn and Cassandra Wilcox, as well as the tolerance of Etta MacLennan, during the writing of this book.

We would like, also, to acknowledge our gratitude to the *Listener* for permission to reproduce part of an article by John Lloyd entitled 'Kill The Chocolate Biscuit', first published in October 1975.

'I Apologize' was written by Hoffman, Goodheart and Nelson. In some of the stories we have changed, or omitted names and details of places and people that might otherwise incriminate them - or us.

The cartoons are by Rod Jordan whose work has enlivened the end credits of all the 'Braden's Week' and 'That's Life' programmes - and has enriched television programmes for millions of viewers.

Contents

Foreword

Like thousands of other married couples we actually enjoy working together. It was work that brought us together in the first place and it has been working with each other that has given us the greatest professional pleasure.

This book might never have been written if it wasn't for an argument that sprang up in the BBC about our working together. It made us think about the problems, as well as the pleasures, of married couples working together.

We thought about it, as often as we could, in between asking a photographer from one newspaper to come out from under the rhododendrons and telling a reporter from another that we weren't quite ready to write the signed story of 'How Our Love and Passion Cost Us Dear'. In any case, it didn't.

But the idea of working together didn't fade – and won't.

We reflected that, between us, we could now add up a whole lifetime of television experience. And what were we going to do about that?

'I remember those long anecdotes and the lengthy location stories you always told at screenings. Actually they held up quite a lot of screenings,' said Esther. 'So now, why don't we write a book together? All your stories and all my stories – what really goes on behind the scenes in television.'

Well, why not? What goes on behind the scenes in television has always seemed rather more amusing, and certainly more revealing, to both of us than much of what we all labour so hard to put in front of the viewers on the screen. It's the rows and the love affairs, it's the famous with their hair down, the mistakes and the bloomers, that really rivet people. The BBC Club, the hotel dining rooms – and the hotel bedrooms – are where some of the best stories happen. Mind you, the boardroom, the Programme Review meeting, the annual interview with one's boss are also moments which the viewers don't normally learn about. And there's still the casting couch. It does indeed exist, a little worn, rather old fashioned and, on the whole these days, used only as a ploy by ageing variety producers auditioning beauty queens, and senior executives with strong show business connections.

It could even be that 'Coronation Street', 'Man Alive', 'This Week' and 'Panorama' may never seem quite the same again once we've finished prattling on. Wouldn't it be nice if that were really so?

But we both agreed we ought to try to write a book intended for pleasure, for the bedside table, the long journey or even the loo (or are we the only couple in the world that keeps a supply of books and magazines in the loo?). Anyway, a book in which we aim to please.

We agreed. Both of us have stories of our own and then there are, as well, the many stories of our friends and colleagues in television. We decided to put them all down, with much gratitude to our friends for allowing us to tell their tales, and some straining of our own memories.

'That's settled then,' Esther said. 'Why don't you write it?'

I did. And we both hope you enjoy it. We've told our stories together the way most married couples do, the way I suspect they have throughout the ages.

You know how it goes. The husband always seems to take over the conversation at the beginning and do most of the talking – but it's usually his wife who caps the story.

And that, more or less, is how we've done it.

Kew, 1981

1 How to get in

The first time we worked together was on a freezing cold night in 1968, in a dark car park by the Serpentine in Hyde Park. 'Braden's Week' had just started and Esther had been picked as one of the two reporter-researchers. I had agreed to direct some of the early film stories.

This was to be Esther's first film and it was nearly her last. There had been a story in the newspapers about a courting couple who had been canoodling in a steamed-up car when a policeman rapped smartly on the windscreen and nearly produced a dangerous spasm in the pair of them. The gentleman in the car had been rather cross and the case had come to court. John Lloyd, the programme producer, thought it would be an interesting idea if we went down to the Serpentine at night where, he had noticed, you could always find at least two dozen steamed-up cars parked under the trees.

'What you ought to do is to tiptoe up with a crew, switch on the battery lights at the last moment, rap on the window and then ask the couple how they would feel if someone rapped on the window,' he said.

Esther looked as if she thought it sounded more like a kamikaze mission than a film assignment.

It was an extremely cold, foggy evening. When we arrived with the film crew at the quiet little row of cars with our dazzling battery lights, stick microphones and the hand-held camera, we were hardly popular. But we pressed on. No power on earth would make Esther confess, on her first film reporting assignment, that she was nervous. We switched on lights, knocked on windows. And, as is proper on these occasions, the reporter – Esther – was in front of all of us, taking the brunt of it. One man opened his door violently, pushing it against Esther, leapt out and started to wrench the microphone out of her hand.

I felt it was time I did something authoritative. I shouted, 'Don't punch her – punch me.' He did.

We switched off the lights and retreated to the bushes for a small council of war. We decided to press on. The story, against all the odds, started to work. In one steamed-up car the rapping on the windows, the lights and the crew were totally ignored. It will take me a long time to forget the image of a shivering Esther Rantzen bent over the windscreen of the car with the standard formal introduction: 'Excuse me, sir and madam, I'm from the BBC.'

An astonishing number of people emerged from the steamed-up interiors, untangling themselves and blinking in the lights, happy to talk to us about how they would have reacted if we hadn't been a film team but a policeman. One man capped them all. 'I'm an off-duty policeman myself,' he said. 'Come in and join me.' We made our excuses and switched off the battery lights.

There were certainly enough amiable, eccentric and witty couples to make a short film (eventually it was transmitted in the first edition of 'Braden's Week' with the music of 'Hello, Young Lovers' playing underneath). Equally certainly, every time we approached a car and Esther bent forward with the microphone to rap on the steamed up windows, we both thought to ourselves, how did we ever get into a lunatic job like this?

The truth about the extraordinary labyrinth, the world behind the television screen, is that some of it is sordid beyond nightmares and some of it – as most of us would like to believe – is glamorous beyond dreams. But we've discovered that, even during the blackest and most disastrous moments, there is always something ludicrous to relieve the horror. And even on the most glamorous occasions there is, invariably, something comic to puncture the tension.

One occasion was the result of an invitation from an elegant old Etonian friend of ours who asked us to be top-table guests – and Esther to make a speech – at a City of London banquet in the Lord Mayor's Mansion House. It was to be a glittering occasion, he told us, attended by many Lords and Ladies, quite a few 'respectable' millionaires, some distinguished academics and members of the theatrical profession. But, our friend warned us, it was a very, very formal occasion.

That raised the problem of what to wear. So we asked, and our friend said crisply, as though we should certainly have known, 'White tie and tails for you, Desmond. Long dress, gloves and tiara for Esther.'

I groaned. It meant a trip to Moss Bros.

Esther groaned louder. 'Where the hell do I find a tiara?' she asked me.

'See if those nice people in BBC costume or props have got any ideas,' I suggested.

They solved the problem for her. They found a tiara among the costumes for the 'Black and White Minstrel Show'. It was made of aluminium wire and large lumps of glass. It was almost convincing if you didn't come closer than three feet. It would have to do. They also came up with a pair of long white gloves and a length of pink knicker elastic to keep the tiara in place.

We arrived at the Mansion House looking like a couple from a Walt Disney extravaganza. I had gone right over the top at Moss Bros. As well as white tie and tails, I had rented a full length opera cloak with a red silk lining, and a top hat.

'All you need is a rabbit – or a pair of doves,' said Esther in the car.

'You look very nice too, darling,' I replied. But revenge was to be mine – and soon.

The occasion really was as glittering as our friend had predicted. The chandeliers glowed and sparkled; in the minstrels' gallery an ensemble of musicians played light classical music; footmen stood in doorways and a major domo bellowed the name of every guest for the benefit of the receiving line. There were several hundred elegant ladies and gentlemen at the banquet. The men were all wearing white tie and tails, complete with medal ribbons, decorations and orders. The ladies were all in long dresses and white gloves. But only one lady was wearing a tiara – Esther.

Full credit to her, she didn't flinch or flee to the powder room to take it off. She adjusted the knicker elastic and strode to the top table on the arm of the host. It gave her something to talk about for the first few minutes of her speech. The men at the banquet looked amused and the ladies sympathetic.

She was coming to the end of her speech and had just begun to wind up with 'thank you for asking us' when there was a sudden noise, a sharp snapping sound. The elastic on her tiara had given way.

Slowly the tiara tilted forward on to her forehead and fell to the table in front of her, where it lay among the coffee cups and glasses in all its glass and bent wire splendour, the pink elastic hanging down over the edge of the table.

There was silence. It was, after all, a very dignified banquet. Thank God, at least Esther had already mentioned the history of the tiara. She saved the moment. 'I'm afraid I've dropped a bit of a bloomer,' she said and sat down.

We didn't really intend to join a kind of British showbusiness Mafia in which power and greed, sex and high living, treachery and betrayal, were as much part of the everyday scene as curling egg sandwiches and powdered milk in the coffee. But then, in 1960, we knew very little about television.

Esther was still at university, cavorting in student revues, hardly thinking of television at all, let alone a career in it. I was, at that time, a newspaper man, nine years in Fleet Street, which meant nine years of travelling round the world. Not a bad life. But it came to an abrupt halt one afternoon when, working a Saturday shift for extra money from the Sunday paper, I was hit on the head with a car bumper jack by a

crook whose photograph we'd 'snatched' earlier that day. I hadn't even written the story myself, just agreed to act as driver for the photographer. The man was the leader of a gang being exposed by the *Sunday Pictorial* for running a racket in which they rounded up pet cats in London suburbs and sold them to vivisection laboratories. It was a story certain to reach the pet-loving hearts of a tabloid reading nation although I lost interest in it when he hit me.

After nearly a year, first without any sight at all, then half-sight, then with whole sight but double vision, and finally with fully restored whole sight, I was freed from the attentions of surgeons, doctors and specialists, ready to return to my craft – scarred but unbowed.

It wasn't that I expected a hero's welcome. After all I had already started telling the story of why they had taken the skin from my behind to graft over the scars on my face. I was proud of the punchline '. . . so you see, I must be the only person you've ever met who can truly be said to speak through a hole in his behind.'

As I say, I wasn't expecting a hero's welcome although a mild ripple of appreciation might have helped. But I had forgotten the News Editor, a man cynically above emotion, desiccated, devoted to a philosophy of remaining unmoved by anything put before him by the reporters. Helping a foreign legionaire escape, smuggling him to Britain and the arms of his society girlfriend produced the response: 'Another love story'. Riding into the Guyanian jungle on a mule for ten days in order to find the front line of a revolutionary war (which other journalists were content to report from the hotel bar) elicited: 'You've been out of touch and spending money, unforgivable'.

So, I suppose I shouldn't have been surprised when he said: 'We thought we'd let your eyes rest a bit. You're on the late shift.' That meant nine p.m. till four a.m., the 'graveyard'. It meant a filthy newsroom, tired sub-editors, drunks on the phone, traffic accidents on the teleprinter and a cold wait for the all-night bus back to North London. It was a salutary reminder – clearly intended – that reporters were humble creatures who should be aware of their place. Back in the newsroom I gazed again at the face of a distinguished journalist who was also sharing the 'graveyard' shift. He was a man who professed to being nearly sixty (I was twenty-nine) and all of us knew that he was at least eight years older than that, determined to keep working, indeed needing to keep working. He was admirable, but was I being shown my own future?

Also that night, I spotted the same advertisement in both the *New Statesman* and *World's Press News* (you have to read something between phone calls from drunks). It read:

> Television reporter wanted for network current affairs ITV magazine programme. Experience, looks, personality essential. Imagination and commitment also essential. Send details and photograph. Box number ...

I didn't actually have a television set but the man who made jug after jug of dark brown tea in the copy boys' corner of the tape room was always talking about his. He helped me work out that the programme concerned was 'This Week'.

The crime photographer was dragged into the secret with the promise of a drink in the Press Club when we both got off duty at four a.m. He took and processed a set of what we both agreed were brilliant photographs. There I was, the poor man's Bogart, wearing a raincoat with the collar turned up (it wasn't even my raincoat) sitting at a desk in a deserted newsroom, leaning on a typewriter and talking on a phone. If you studied the print carefully it was just possible to make out, free of raincoat, typewriter or telephone, the whole of one eye and part of my mouth.

In an attempt to beat the obedient applicants who would reply to the box number, I gambled that we were right and sent the photograph and a rather arrogant application directly to 'This Week' (I was deeply under the influence of Philip Marlowe and Lew Archer at the time and most of my writing then reflected the 'down-these-mean-streets-a-man-must-go' style).

We had guessed right, the tape room man and I. I was invited for an interview.

Arriving at Television House, Kingsway I was asked by a receptionist whose eyes I never saw - I didn't have time to pan up from my inspection of her astonishing cleavage - to take the lift to the first floor where I was expected in the 'Green Room'.

After twenty minutes of wandering the corridors of the first floor, where all the doors were red, I knocked in desperation on any door only to learn my first lesson in television vocabulary. The Green Room, it turned out, had a number and wasn't green. It was named after the room used in the theatre as a place where the actors can relax.

I went to it. It had double doors opening inwards. I flung them open trying to feel like a confident athlete about to bang J. Arthur Rank's gong. I was unprepared for a number of things. Firstly, the four men and one woman interview panel were facing the double doors in a half circle, gazing at the empty chair I was to occupy. For reasons best known to them, they were in semi-darkness.

The double doors were hung in a recess below floor level involving a step up into the Green Room, which in the half darkness, I didn't see. I fell full-length on the carpet, in front of Associated Rediffusions' Interviewer selection board, scraping my cheekbone on the back of the candidate's chair as I went down.

Only slightly muffled by the fact that my mouth was buried in the carpet, I spoke my first words in the company of distinguished television executives. 'What a bloody stupid way to hang a door.'

The lady turned out to be an executive in Features and was, I learned later, capable of out-swearing a Marine drill sergeant. She slapped her tweed-clad thigh like a principal boy in panto – honestly she did – and said: 'He'll do, by God he'll do.' She didn't speak again. I learned later that she seldom did after lunch. I then staggered through a series of questions from the Head of Features, the Controller of Programmes and the producer of 'This Week'. Long afterwards I discovered we were talking two different languages and I am forever grateful that their misunderstanding seemed to work in my favour.

'Do you think you can manage a story a week?' they asked me.

'One a week? I'm used to doing three or four a day,' I replied.

I don't think they believed me, although it was true. But then I didn't realize that what they meant was research, travel, film, travel, cut, dub and transmit a film story of ten minutes or more in length; a good week's work in television.

'Auditions. Downstairs. Half an hour. Shortlisted three hundred, interviewed thirty, test the last six,' they said in their own form of shorthand.

I didn't understand a word, it was all magic. But I had begun to sweat. Where was downstairs? Was it another myth like the Green Room? Perhaps on the sixth floor? And what kind of doors would this room have?

Downstairs turned out to be a studio. Cameras, lights, men and women with headphones, disembodied voices speaking from the ceiling and sounding like slightly common gods. Why was it necessary to boom 'Good luck, studio' to all this inanimate equipment? I waited in what was called a dressing room. Five other candidates waited in five other dressing rooms.

My turn came. I had adjusted the knot in my tie so frequently that when the incredibly beautiful secretary sent to fetch me said, 'Follow me', I could only manage a strangled squeak. She led me through the darkness into a pool of light facing a television camera. A man in headphones was standing alongside it, as though he was about to put children on top of it and take them for a ride round the zoo. He said, 'Look into the lens.' It was like being x-rayed. Then he said: 'Wait for the red light and then speak clearly and without hesitation about your ideas to fill this week's "This Week" with a running order drawn from the headlines of this morning's newspapers. Counting now. Nine, eight, seven, six, five, four, three ...'

It was impossible to resist. It never fails. Why the space-ships of NASA do not take off semi-flooded and rusting from the triggered release of overtensed bladders caused by this kind of countdown I'll never know. All I knew at the time was I needed to be anywhere other than gazing into the lens, waiting for the red light and listening to this highly-paid torturer count backwards from ten.

Under this new and painful pressure, I spoke more quickly than I ever have in my life before. I recalled instantly the five main news stories of the day, dismissed two of them as impossibly expensive to cover, commented that the third would probably be boring, but had to be done, and suggested that the final two offered a contrast in styles; one was an interview with a man who had twice been sentenced to death and, now released, was trying to sell his story; and the other, I suggested, could be an interview with a then little-heard-of Anglican Bishop who had just been bounced out of Africa because he had correctly learned how to pronounce the word apartheid. ('Remember,' he told reporters, 'Apartheid rhymes with hate.') He had also, incautiously, told the auth-orities what he thought (and what any good Christian should think) of South Africa's separatist policies.

'He would be good to interview,' I said. 'Because he's already learned that newsmen aren't like congregations. Now he says it all briefly and puts the main point in the first paragraph.'

I was going to go on. But a sudden pang from my bladder made me stop – abruptly.

Later, they told me they admired my professional tech-nique, they liked interviewers who spoke briefly, to the point – and then shut up. I could have explained – but I decided to shut up.

The voice of God boomed out again from the loudspeakers hidden in the darkness above the studio lights.

'All right, now here's what I want you to discuss in one minute, twenty-five seconds,' it said in the kind of per-emptory tone that I know for certain will greet me from St Peter's loudspeaker if ever I'm allowed even to approach those pearly gates. 'Explain the Birmingham bus boycott. Simple language please.'

I did so briefly, mentioned Martin Luther King, suggested that the civil rights demonstration at that moment going on in Birmingham, Alabama would in time reverberate round the world and that skulls being broken by policemen's batons at the time would certainly become the heroic folklore of a massive campaign. I stopped. I was finished. But were they? I was in agony.

The beautiful girl emerged, even more languidly, from the darkness as I stood, by now, literally on one leg. 'I'll take you back to your dressing room. They've one other candidate and then they'll let you know,' she said. Could I tell this elegant creature about my base needs? My nerve failed. I hobbled after her.

Shut in the dressing room, alone at last, gasping as though I had just been thrown back in my cell after an interrogation by the KGB, I discovered another, older, theatrical truth.

The dressing room had a wash hand basin. And I did not have the nerve to leave the dressing room to go in search ...

I can't have been the first and I'm sure I'm not going to be the last. When the languid lady returned I was beaming with pleasure and relief. 'You're all to wait in dressing room six,' she said.

In dressing room six I found the five other candidates I had not met before. One was a lady colleague from a Fleet Street newspaper. The others were unknown to me. We edged round each other like terriers meeting in the park, offered cigarettes, sprang to click lighters for each other and spoke with cynical, disparaging jokiness about the audition we'd just been through, looking carefully, nevertheless, for hidden microphones, just in case.

The producer of 'This Week' at that time was bearded, forceful, dynamic. (I know he was dynamic because he always told me so.) He bustled into the room.

'Thank you all very much, you can all go now except Mr Wilcox, I'd like him to come upstairs and meet the Head of Features. Incidentally,' he said to the lady journalist, 'the

Birmingham bus boycott isn't "some kind of silly industrial action on the buses in the Midlands", so do go and read your papers, dear.' And he bustled out.

'Jesus,' said one of the men, whose face I was beginning to recognize as familiar from the cigarette commercials I most admired.

'Oh stuff him. And sod television too. I'll bet it won't last,' said the lady journalist, stubbing her cigarette out on the polished surface of the dressing table, bursting into tears and running from the room.

The rest all looked at me. It was a long moment and clearly I, also, was expected to display some kind of emotion. I considered telling them that I, too, was scandalized by the brutality of the producer's behaviour, and that I certainly wasn't going to take any job that might be offered me.

It was also clear that at least two of them would then have volunteered immediately to replace me.

'The hell with it,' I said, with an attempt at lightness. 'I might as well go and find out what they think they're doing. Funny world this . . .'

I left, as quickly as I decently could, while I still remained in their minds as, only possibly, the most hated man in the world. Another two minutes and it would have been a certainty.

Upstairs in the Green Room again they offered me a thirteen week contract. (Why thirteen? Is it lucky for some, I thought? I didn't know then that all television existed in the American pattern and reflected the year's quarters.) They also offered £12 a week more than I was getting in Fleet Street and they clearly weren't going to give me time to consider. But £12 a week was a fortune. You know, a bunch of flowers, theatre, dinner for two, hotel for the night, taxi home, and still have change to get to work in the morning . . .

I said 'Yes' and left to give in my notice to the *Daily Mirror*, after ten years a solemn moment. The crime photographer made me buy him yet another drink. He said it must have been his photograph that did it. It might well have been, at that. It seemed a mad enough world.

Thirteen weeks after I joined, the same producer recommended against renewing my contract. I'd learned a lot by then – some of the lessons are in the rest of this book – but I still fail to understand one of his reasons for wanting me out. He told the Head of Features that he never really trusted men who wore brown shoes. Sadly I went home, mentally composing a letter to the Editor of the *Daily Mirror* which started, 'If you will forgive my recent madness . . .'

Back at 'This Week' the next day I discovered that the Head of Features had removed the producer of 'This Week', shifted him to other programmes. I was reprieved. Later the Head of Features was removed himself. If I'd thought Fleet Street was a rough place, I hadn't begun to understand the meaning of 'long knives', until I reached television.

At least my first audition opened the doors of television. Esther's first audition nearly closed the doors on her for good.

She was working in radio in 1965, not as a presenter or performer, but as a studio manager. She was, for a while, the sound effects on 'Mrs Dale's Diary', rattling tea cups, telephone bells, doors opening and shutting. She worked on other radio plays too, and even invented sound effects; the flapping of a pterodactyl's wings swooping towards its victim in the steaming jungles of prehistoric earth. No one challenged the accuracy of her new skill. After all, who knows what a pterodactyl's wings really sounded like? She did it, incidentally, by opening and shutting a gent's umbrella in front of the microphone. It ruined the umbrella but kept the younger listeners delightedly terrified.

That job came to a head when one lady drama producer who may, or may not, have been a sadist but grimly confessed to being a perfectionist, decided that the only accurate way to reproduce the sound of a falling body was for Esther's to be the body doing the falling – on to the parquet floor of the studio. In search of the precise sound the producer decided to record the effect over and over again. Bruised and disillusioned, the young Rantzen groaned her way up from the floor after the fourteenth attempt had been pronounced 'just acceptable' and went in search of writing paper in order to resign.

But before her resignation one of her honorary aunts – the Rantzen family have a number of these, even though they're not short of the real kind – an author and lecturer at Cambridge University, had seen an advertisement in a local paper for a new 'Miss Romper Room' to work on Anglia Television's children's programme. She suggested Esther should apply. They sent her a train ticket to go and audition in Norwich.

In the studios a collection of well-groomed, nervous ladies stood around waiting for somebody to speak to them. In another corner of the same studio a rather doleful group of children, aged from four to eight, stood looking as though they'd done it all before. They had. They were the 'live' audience which the potential Miss Romper Rooms were expected to charm and amuse.

One at a time, the girls were invited to step forward, read a little introduction from the autocue on the camera and then tell a fairy story to the group of children who, by now, were looking quite glassy-eyed.

Hardened comedians, bloodied in the Glasgow Empire, unafraid of the Newcastle Dolce Vita, have been known to run sobbing from the prospect of trying to liven up an audience of tired toddlers.

It was Esther's turn. She read her introduction on the autocue. 'Now,' said the lady producer brightly. 'Tell them the story of Little Red Riding Hood.' Esther plunged in.

'Red Riding Hood was a pretty little blonde girl who went for a walk in the woods one day and met a wolf. Lucky old her ...'

The camera crew giggled and the first sign of animation crossed the faces of her childish audience. The lady producer appeared as though catapulted. 'Thank you, dear. That's very good,' she said.

The children voted for 'Auntie' Esther but they were over-ruled. The lady in charge of 'Romper Room' was an American and puritan. She wished Esther good luck in 'whatever she decided to do'. As long as it was somewhere else. I believe it was a loss for Anglia's children. But in the end it was to be this country's consumers' gain.

The one audition in which Esther succeeded with flying colours was one she never wanted to pass – the time she became a white slave. As her boss, I thought white slavery was a good subject to investigate. As it happened Esther was the only researcher free to investigate it. When I stuck my head round her office door and called out 'white slavery' she looked at me as though I was trying to get rid of her. I nearly succeeded, too. Ten years later she married me which, I suppose, serves me right.

Anyway, I briefed her to find out if it would make a good investigation for 'Braden's Week'. Esther obediently rang up the Salvation Army and asked if they'd rescued any white slaves recently. They'd met people like Esther before and they didn't blink, just suggested she might like to meet their expert on vice, Major Mary Scott.

Major Scott was a marvellous woman, short, rosy-cheeked, modest and full of laughter. She was also the expert investigator of the vice rackets that were flourishing in the West End at the time. She got to know all the girls well and they had come to treat her as a friend. One of the call girls controlled by the most vicious vice kings in Soho at the time, the Messina brothers, even took refuge with her when she was in danger.

It was all very interesting but it wasn't white slavery. Major Scott said Esther should go to Equity for advice. They told her to buy the latest copy of the *Stage*, the theatrical newspaper which, at that time, was full of adverts recruiting girls for 'exciting revues, touring abroad, dancers needed, no experience necessary'. Mrs Priscilla Meredith at Equity said they were having a lot of trouble with dancers sent overseas to the Middle East countries. Many of the girls were tempted to go out there without proper contracts. They would find their hotel bills mounting up, then discover that their passports had disappeared. Then, the nightclub owner would tell them that their only way out of this dilemma was to do a lot more than dancing.

So, 'Why not do an audition yourself?' Mrs Meredith suggested to Esther.

'Have you seen me dance?' Esther said.

'I promise you, even if you had three heads and a wooden leg you'd still be taken on, just as long as you're female,' said Mrs Meredith.

Esther went for an audition. So did John Pitman, her fellow reporter on Braden's Week. Not because he also wanted to be a white slave, but because Esther's mother insisted. She said she'd read about girls being surreptitiously injected with strange drugs, rolled up in carpets and bundled away never to be seen again outside the walls of the casbah. Esther's mother was adamant that Bernard Braden and I should send somebody to wait outside during the audition – and check every bundle of laundry that went in and out.

John Pitman was elected. Esther's audition was with a Mr Taki Bengali. That wasn't his real name of course, his real name was Pan Theodossiou, and he was President of the United Arab Republic Magic Circle. By then nothing could surprise Esther. Before she even sang to him, Taki Bengali, as he preferred to be known in Soho, explained to Esther that he hired girls to 'consummate'.

There was a long pause during which Esther claims she could sense John Pitman – sitting on the stairs outside the audition hall – bristling with Bulldog Drummond readiness to do a heroic rescue. Then Taki Bengali explained that 'consummation' is a technical term for drinking with the customers. Taki went on: 'In the club you dance and then you consummate. You like consummating?' There was no answer to that. 'After the show,' he said, 'the customers ask you to join them. They order the champagne, they drink the champagne and you drink the coloured water. You get commission from every bottle you have consummated.' Taki Bengali's explanation was interrupted by the phone. Mr Bengali started to bellow into it.

It turned out to be Esther's mother who'd rung to make sure she was all right. Now that's the kind of thing that doesn't happen to Charlie's Angels. It's a bit demeaning to have your cover blown by your mother – but understandable, once you've met Esther's mother. Esther managed to reassure her mother, apologize to Taki Bengali, agree that she now understood the meaning of consummation and hand her sheet music to the pianist who was waiting for the audition to begin.

The song she'd chosen was 'I can't give you anything but love'. She asked the pianist for the lowest key he could find and proceeded to blast her way through it. John Pitman, waiting outside, couldn't believe it. The volume was immense – he said it was like the love call of the great white whale. Even Taki backed away as far as the window, until Esther finished. Then he said 'How old are you?'

'Twenty-six,' Esther lied, lopping off two years.

Even then he didn't look too pleased – twenty-six was obviously rather mature for the customers at the Kit-Kat club in Beirut. But, as the Equity lady had said, even though Esther was elderly and baritone she was at least female.

'I pay you £20 a week,' said Taki (that would be £50 today). 'We leave in three weeks.'

Esther said she'd think it over. John Pitman didn't have to dash in from the stairs to make an heroic rescue. Later Esther rang the Foreign Office who told her about the sad little girls who were turning up on the steps of Embassies all over the Middle East, in debt to their management, their passports confiscated by the club owner. A year later 'Braden's Week' had to fly a girl back from the Middle East to tell the viewers how she had been trapped the same way.

The *Stage* and other theatrical newspapers have tightened up their regulations now and will only accept advertisers who offer Equity-approved contracts. But it seems that the white slavers still stalk our cities, because only a short while ago Esther and I read another investigation. And there he was – still indefatigably 'consummating' – our own Mr Taki Bengali. By now we'd both become a little fond of him; after all, he did once try to hire the voice of the great white whale, who later became my wife.

Auditions are one way in but, of course, it's not unknown for people to 'get in' to the BBC or ITV companies via dinners, lunches, relatives and string-pulling contacts. Some young hopefuls practise considerable ingenuity and imagination in wording the letter that will draw the notice of a producer, or polishing the phrase that will make a director listen during dinner.

Yet another route, from Oxbridge. Esther and I have, from time to time, received that most flattering of all kinds of invitation, to speak at a Cambridge, or Oxford, Union debate. I find it more flattering than Esther because I didn't go to university, I didn't even survive the sixth form, and I've always been in awe of university life of any kind, let alone the privileged Oxbridge atmosphere.

So there I was, on a train on my way to Cambridge, with my dinner jacket in a polythene bag on the luggage rack and a scribbling pad full of half-finished, convoluted, highly literate witticisms on my knee. The proposition was that 'This country gets the press it deserves' and I was defending journalism as a profession by attacking gossip columnists and the gutter press. I did so well that I produced the biggest victory for the other side recorded for some years. I had, too, missed the main purpose behind my invitation.

An officer of the Union, let's call him Dazzlebit, was a good-looking, confident, fair-haired product of the prep and public school system who had probably been captain of the school cricket team and was undoubtedly loved by the lower school. Over the brown windsor soup and the congealing lamb chops, he spoke admiringly of the programmes for which I was responsible in the BBC. He'd done his homework well, he poured the flattery on with a heavy hand, undiluted as honey from the pot.

I fell for it like Winnie the Pooh, who was, as we all remember, a bear of little brain.

When young Dazzlebit mentioned his desire to join the BBC, 'but only if I could work on stimulating and provocative programmes like yours', I arranged for him to be interviewed. He sailed through a whole series of BBC Boards as to the manner born. He and the BBC were clearly made for each other.

'Getting in' is also a matter of luck. The ambitious may travel schemingly but the lucky, even the unconcerned, are just as likely to arrive too.

James Cameron, whom I have always regarded as my journalistic godfather, was, by 1963, the veteran of many brilliant commentaries for television documentaries. But he had never considered appearing in vision when we both went to Washington to report, for 'This Week' the biggest civil rights demonstration the United States had ever seen.

A quarter of a million people moved purposefully up past the Reflecting Pools to gather round the marble feet of Abraham Lincoln, seated frozen-faced in his memorial.

On 'This Week' we were covering the event by satellite, an adventurous experiment. The main speaker was Martin Luther King Jr, a leader and hero for all the civil rights workers and a man who had marched many hundreds of miles at risk of his life, leading columns of protesters.

He had twelve minutes before he was due to address the huge audience. Jeremy Isaacs, the producer in London, suggested a quick interview. I agreed and countered with the suggestion that James Cameron had logged up nearly as much bone-aching mileage as Martin Luther King in the name of one sort of humanitarian protest or another, so perhaps he would be much more qualified than me for the job of interviewer even though it would be his debut.

Minutes later, seated knee to knee, on folding metal chairs in a 'studio' created by the shadow of Abraham Lincoln's behind, the great civil rights leader and the veteran journalist campaigner were waiting to be cued on to the satellite transmission to Britain. I was doing the cueing.

'Are you sure this is wise, Desmond?' Jimmy was asking me

over Martin Luther King's shoulder as the voice in my headphones from London said, 'Take Washington'. I could only nod vigorously, so vigorously that my headphones fell off.

It was not so much an interview, more an exchange of seasoned protesters' anecdotes. Jimmy started unhesitatingly. 'Now, I don't know if I've walked as many miles as you but I think I've covered rather more causes, and this whole business of wearing out shoe leather in order to achieve political ambition becomes absolutely secondary to the pain of wondering whether your feet will last, when your varicose veins are going to develop, and how you're ever going to get through another day of it. Don't you find that the physical weariness almost submerges the political belief, after a while, so that when you come to a village or a town and they're waving a flag, or a banner, it's something of a shock to be reminded that you're here for a purpose? And I've always found . . .'

At this point Martin Luther King, smiling more broadly than I'd ever seen, leaned forward and grasped Jimmy Cameron by the knee. He looked at him with huge affection. 'You're so right,' he said. 'So right. Just let me tell you . . .'

And between them these two admirable veterans of Christian causes capped each other's marching stories until the time, all too soon, ran out. Martin Luther King had been interviewed many times already. There were more occasions to come, but I still regard that affectionate, idiosyncratic conversation as one of the most enduring and endearing of my memories of the great civil rights leader.

Twenty minutes after that interview, Martin Luther King made his speech and coined for the first time the phrase that was to become the heroic rallying cry of his movement, 'I have a dream . . .'

Once upon a time, there was a nice little old lady living alone in a London flat, who used to go to a hospital in Fulham every Monday to receive out-patient therapy for her arthritis.

She was a spry, bright-eyed, inquisitive old lady who invariably wore a turban style hat and a neat woollen coat. She'd been a widow for eight years, lived alone with her memories and occasional visits from her son and daughter, both married and living out of London.

As she wandered through the North End Road market, she spotted a crowd, a big one. Thinking it might be a fight or a row – she liked watching both – the little old lady went to investigate. It was, in fact, 'That's Life!' at work.

Esther was filming in the market, as she does nearly every Monday, the 'vox pops' that have taken on more the atmosphere of a street carnival than a serious current affairs inquiry. They were, as usual, testing something obscure – this time they wanted to know if people could tell the difference between champagne and cider.

The little old lady took to the camera like a veteran. Thorndyke or Dame Edith couldn't have done it better. Penelope Keith or Beryl Reid couldn't have timed it more precisely.

'Well,' she said slowly. 'Usually I only drink freemans.'

'What's that?' said Esther.

'You know, freemans, the drink you don't pay for,' she replied. 'I must try again.' She did. 'Again.'

Esther was beginning to cotton on. 'Can't you tell by now?' she asked.

'Well all freemans tastes delicious,' said Annie Mizzen – little knowing that she was starting on the path to television fame.

Told it was champagne, she uttered a delighted 'Ooh', winked at the camera like an old trouper and helped herself to another glass.

The following week they were out in the streets again – and they met Annie again. She tasted caviare for the first time.

'That's just like mouse's droppings,' she said as she helped herself to another dollop.

By the third week, when she had dangled a diminutive squid in front of her and said, 'just like my old man's doodahs', we all knew a star had been discovered.

People have often suggested that Annie was sent for from a theatrical agency, recruited from a seaside troupe, or paid for her regular appearances in 'That's Life!'. None of this is true. She always happened to be in the market place on her way for hospital treatment at the time regularly chosen for the film crew to shoot. She liked them, and they liked her, and on the one day that she didn't appear it caused consternation and many phone calls before we discovered where she lived and reassured ourselves.

After that the crew would always say, 'See you next week', and Annie would always be there. Sadly she is no longer strong enough to make it, and at ninety she is enjoying her memories of television stardom in a convalescent home in Essex. She phones us regularly and always watches the street interviews with an expert eye.

Few viewers would have guessed that the pert, saucy little lady in those street situations was in fact a whole story in herself. As a young girl at school she sailed through exam after exam and was encouraged by her teacher to stay on after fourteen and become a teacher herself. Her parents simply couldn't afford it, she had to leave school. So Annie worked as a cleaner for most of her life. But she saw to it that her children had a full education and always relished the fact that her own daughter became a teacher.

Her daughter, in turn, loved the fact that her mother was now in television, a star.

2 How to get on

His Royal Highness Prince Philip, the Duke of Edinburgh, was becoming irritable with our film team. I could tell that quite clearly, watching the film 'rushes' in our viewing room.

But the regal scowl, the irritable glance directly at the camera, which has been known to make more establishment-minded film crews and journalists at home in England quail with terror and retreat, for fear that their bosses' knighthoods might be endangered was not working. In Texas the subtle methods of communicating royal displeasure weren't known and – I'm glad to say – the BBC film crew who, perhaps, should have known better consisted of a brilliant but irreverent Australian cameraman, Butch Calderwood, and a dedicated and single-minded sound man called Don Martin.

The Duke was 'going West' – travelling round the Western part of the United States, piloting a British aeroplane, reinforcing British commercial prestige, and generally showing the flag where sometimes Presidents feared to tread. And 'Man Alive' was going with him. We had permission to travel on the royal plane, interview His Highness at the controls and bring back a half-hour film about our democratic Prince mixing with millionaires and multi-millionaires almost as though they were ordinary people, or he was ordinary people, or nobody was rich, or something like that. The 'Man Alive' programme was to be called 'The Duke Goes West' and the reason for this anecdote in this particular chapter is that the lesson I learned from that royal trip was that it was really my career that was going west, not the Queen's husband.

You can't blame the film crew, indeed they should be praised for their imaginative coverage. Only minutes before, a dozen plump and rouged Southern matrons, dressed in more flowing chiffon than ever took to the 'Come Dancing' floor, had nervously approached our camera crew while they were filming to ask burning questions on the matter of protocol.

'How do you curtsey without falling flat on your fanny?' asked one ample lady wearing enough diamonds to make an oil sheik blink.

To his credit the admirable Don Martin, gun mike in hand, headphones on ears, Nagra recorder round his neck, curtsied. And to his credit – and our delight – Butch Calderwood filmed him doing it. The unexpected vision of a BBC sound man teaching a billion dollars' worth of Texan ladies how to curtsey was a golden moment. Clearly, this also put him on intimate terms with them all. He had become a friend, almost a dance teacher. He was expected to stay and he did.

The Duke arrived. His plane blew all the back-combed hairstyles out flat. His royal manner, aristocratic charm and British sex appeal bowled the matrons even flatter. They curtsied perfectly and gathered round him as though scrummaging for the rugby ball in the England–Wales match. At any moment one expected to see him 'heeled' out of the back row of the scrum, grabbed by a pink skirted scrum half and passed down the three-quarters, maybe even carried over the line for a try.

Into this scrummage plunged Don Martin, gun mike rampant, to record the 'oohing' and 'aahing' and the 'How is your son Chuck?' conversation. The ladies parted to allow him proper access. He was, after all, their friend and dancing master. Don's eyes switched between the conversation and his recording dial. He clearly didn't recognize the royal storm warnings.

So, it was as he pushed the microphone even closer that he received, at full volume, the royal command: 'Why don't you take that thing and stuff it right up ...'

That moment did more to 'de-stuff' the British image in Texas and increase our trading prospects in America than all the Embassy cocktail parties put together. The atmosphere in our darkened viewing room warmed up. It was going to be a good film.

It never occurred to me for one moment that elsewhere in the BBC there would be wise and experienced men, sanguine leaders, veterans of the political tightrope act, executives who might think otherwise. I was, after all, concerned with getting on with my job, making a good programme, attracting viewers, keeping them informed and entertained, getting better coverage than other programmes. But 'getting on', really 'getting on', is about climbing within the organization – not necessarily making programmes well.

When 'Man Alive: The Duke Goes West' was broadcast, I was quite pleased at the stir it caused. There we were, in every newspaper, on the front pages of quite a few, with headlines like; 'The Duke says "stuff it"'. And they all spelled the name of the programme right and raced off to the airport to meet the Duke, who was due to arrive back from his tour the day after the broadcast.

In the VIP lounge at London's Heathrow Airport the Duke had agreed to a press conference. With his advisers and the business experts who'd flown with him on his successful tour, he was no doubt prepared to elaborate on the nature of his achievement, the amount of business generated and the commercial prospects still to be developed.

But, in the sort of chorus that small boys in the Lower Remove adopt when they're trying to tell 'Sir' that Smith Minor was responsible for the rude drawing on the blackboard, the press of Great Britain, as one man, wanted only to know: 'Why did you tell the BBC to stuff it?'

The Duke grinned broadly and carried off the moment, as he often does when recalling his altercations with the media, with humour. 'They were getting in the way and I knew that would stop them from broadcasting what they were listening to,' he said, perhaps speculating for a fraction of a second on why it was that so many press men seemed to know about this obscure moment two weeks ago in the heartland of Texas. Before he could speculate further, he received his answer.

'Oh, but they did broadcast it,' came back the chorus of press.

'Ah,' said the Duke.

My boss at the BBC said rather more. He wore a monocle and was, at that time, famous for the distinguished sports and outside broadcast programmes in his charge, many of them introduced by him personally. He was affluent, smooth, intelligent, educated and a totally admirable member of the establishment. Spread on the desk in front of him were the newspapers.

For the second day running my newly invented 'Man Alive' was on the front pages – all the front pages. The pleasure I felt at this achievement began to dim as the thought entered my mind that my boss didn't share my delight in the programme and the press coverage it had received.

Half an hour later, when I had not spoken a word and my boss had hardly seemed to pause for breath, I was in possession of the full text of my first Corporation lesson in 'getting on'. 'Offend not the mighty' is, perhaps, too easy a description. It should be: 'Anything you do or say is bound to offend someone and, if they are mighty, then the kicks will go all the way round the circle before winding up on your own arse.'

The second part of the lesson could be: 'Royalty may have a sense of humour but those close to them seldom do. So, never take the mickey out of Royalty.'

In case I had not properly learned the lesson from the extended flow of carefully chosen, never-a-word-repeated invective, as well as the carefully considered forecast of my own future, there was to be the final, crushing, humiliation – the ultimate in BBC exile.

'And,' added my boss, 'you are certainly not welcome in the BBC box at Ascot this year!'

Actually, I didn't even know the BBC maintained a box at Ascot for entertaining the famous and the useful outside the Corporation, and the faithful and friendly inside. I never came out of the doghouse sufficiently long to visit it.

It doesn't necessarily follow that you can only get on by crawling and fawning, or that journalistic enterprise is a handicap. But it often seems like it. I think the real problem is that in large organizations the tremors of everyday life in the front line of the organization, rows with politicians, punch ups with policemen, arguments with establishment figures become magnified, the higher up the organization they are heard – and it sounds like the thunder of doom to the executive at the very top.

So making the wrong kind of noise is a 'snake' and receiving the right kind of praise is a 'ladder' in the game called 'getting on'. I once received a telegram of praise which very nearly made up for all the damage I'd done to the BBC OBEs and CBEs in the offing with my Duke of Edinburgh programme. We'd made a programme about sex education, how young it should start – and why not younger? 'That's it,' I thought. 'It'll be curtains for us now. I expect they'll have the Corporation guillotine polished and ready in the morning.' I was wrong.

Mary Whitehouse sent a telegram, reminding the Director-General (she never thought it worthwhile to send telegrams much below that level) that she once had been a teacher herself and wished to draw his attention to the previous night's 'Man Alive' on sex. What's more, she wished to praise it without reservation. The best of its kind ever made, an ideal for all producers unfortunately usually more concerned with salacious content and sensational headlines.

I was told about the telegram by an august person in Broadcasting House, who is usually described as being 'close' to the Director-General. What the production team and I had considered might be a stimulating and thought-

37

provoking exercise had clearly missed its target. 'Oh God. If Mary Whitehouse likes it, it must have pulled its punches.'

By messenger later that day a short note arrived from the Director-General. 'Very well done. Keep it up, you're clearly right on target.'

My co-editor on 'Man Alive', Bill Morton, a lovely but somewhat gloomy lifelong friend (we never knew whether to be pleased or outraged at the discovery that our team had nicknamed me Winnie the Pooh and him Eeyore) is a mild and unextravagant man. That day he took me to the Club and ordered large whiskies.

Do 'Yes men' succeed? I had always thought not, trustingly believing that those in charge of bright and intelligent people had to be brighter and more intelligent and, therefore, perfectly well able to spot a sycophantic creep a mile off. I was wrong again.

Another rule for 'getting on' in any huge corporation could read: 'Vanity swells in direct proportion to seniority. At the top the capacity for absorbing praise is almost infinite.'

Even the heaviest barrage will succeed; the unashamed declaration, man to man, underling to boss, sycophant to dictator, of admiration and respect. 'I just want to tell you that the BBC's a better place now,' or 'Thank God for you,' or 'It all came from a brilliant remark of yours the other night.'

I knew from watching it in action that this incredible overkill was actually the most successful kind. But when my turn came I used to get seasick, my childhood stutter would return – I just couldn't do it. Worse, although I did admire my bosses in many ways, why did I always wind up telling them I thought they were wrong? The steadfast Bill Morton went through a whole period of buying me whisky in the Club.

'Getting on' ought to be a fair process, a just process, seen to be just. They have, at least, tried to make it so but they don't always succeed. It was the Civil Service that gave television (first the BBC then ITV) the 'Board' system. Getting better jobs is mostly these days promotion via a formal interview in front of a panel of bosses, Boards.

Boards are hell, a hangover from the Spanish Inquisition with the menacing overtones of induction into Freemasonry or the Ku Klux Klan. I have both performed in front of and served on Boards and serving as a member of a Board is nearly as hellish as being one of the candidates. I used to think all other serving members must feel the same, but I reckoned without the fact that the latent sadism in many television executives needs regular expression. Naturally, therefore, the BBC holds a lot of Boards.

And women, who aren't good at what amounts to intellectual gang-bangs, tend to do very badly as candidates, indeed some of them burst into tears. Esther believes that it is because they're too well brought up to use the masculine outlet of a string of four-letter words, once the door is closed behind them – or go off and drown their sorrows in a sea of scotch. All this produces pressure and sometimes tears.

One fine and talented woman producer, a friend of Esther's, in the BBC Current Affairs Group used to arrive confidently in front of the gathering of executives for a promotion board. No matter what they said to her – or what she had told herself before – she burst into tears. Almost as soon as her behind hit the interview chair she would dissolve in muffled sobs. Eventually, they recognized the cruelty of what they were doing, acknowledged her talent and put themselves and her out of their misery by giving her the job on the basis of her track record, regardless of her sobs.

I used to carry a spare handkerchief in case that sort of thing happened when I was serving on a Board. Mind you, women at Boards have sometimes left me more in need of the spare handkerchief for my own use.

One occasion was in a department I ran for the BBC where a list of hopeful candidates were expected to prove, in twenty fast minutes, to a handful of tired and irritable men, that they were ready to pass on from being researchers and become junior directors. There were ten hopefuls on the shortlist and just one job available. The mathematics were certain to create nothing but frustration among the staff. But the manners of the Corporation had to prevail. The most senior man on the Board was large and powerful in every way. He's since gone on to become even more large and powerful.

A pretty girl who'd been working hard on 'The World About Us' series for years and felt, probably rightly, that the producer was exploiting her without promotion, was one of the candidates. And the senior man, in a wise and kindly attempt to broaden the basis of the questions and answers, had been asking everybody what their hobbies were. It was a thoughtful gesture from a senior executive trying to relax the candidates. When her turn came, the lady announced that her hobby was cooking. Then she was asked what she'd done that week. She was expected by the Board to describe her working week on 'The World About Us'. But she said:

'On Monday I cooked my boyfriend a Greek moussaka, and I served it with garlic bread and rough red wine. Then on Tuesday I made a haddock souffle served with a good hock. On Wednesday we were going to eat "out" but then we decided to eat "in" so I had to get something out of the freezer . . .'

Her voice trailed away . . . The large BBC executive appeared to be having a silent fit. Other members of the Board had their eyes fixed on distant points and their face muscles rigidly controlled. A long pause. Finally, words emerged from the great man: 'Sod all that,' he said, startling all of us for, although he was known for making much noise, he was not normally a man given to bad language. 'I want to know about your working week.'

She was a bright and intelligent girl and realized immediately that she'd made a mistake. But she was also an argumentative girl and she couldn't stop herself responding to his last point.

'Oh, but cooking is work. It takes imagination and intelligence. What's more, if you get the diet balance wrong you'll just become fat and disagreeable . . .' She trailed off again.

The great man was, we on the Board all knew, starting his twenty-ninth new diet, in an attempt to reduce the impressive bulk which stood as a living monument to scores of BBC expense account lunches. There were no further exchanges.

Later, much later, she got the job she wanted by talking quietly and hesitantly – at another Board – about the items that had taken her attention in the morning papers and the current biography that she thought might make interesting television.

I, personally, was deeply disappointed. I always wanted to know what it was she would have taken out of the freezer to keep her boyfriend warm on Wednesday night.

The other side to Boards is sitting on them as part of the panel. If there are many candidates, for several jobs, a Board can last for days; eight hours a day, broken remorselessly into twenty-five minute segments. The effect can be disastrous. I once had to be woken up when my turn came to ask questions of a candidate. Fortunately, the interviewee was a woman who had already proved herself by her talented work for me and she got the job. But she has never allowed me to forget that I fell asleep in the middle of her key performance.

The way the candidates dress at Boards is part of the ritual. Would-be creative geniuses wear scuffed plimsolls and pornographic T-shirts. Hopeful young executives wear something safe and sombre. Women find the choice of clothes just as tricky a tightrope. The general opinion seems to be that, in spite of the still very evident prejudice against women in the BBC, the wise ones wear a demure but clinging dress, and cross and uncross their legs quite often. However a cleavage is to be avoided. Too unsubtle.

Among men I've always found that you can tell when they're due for a Board because they arrive dressed as though for a funeral, usually in a dark suit with thin lapels, a tired white shirt and a rather stringy tie. Quite often it seems to be the same suit and tie. I think it is – quick changes in the gents have now become part of the promotion process.

There are quite a few bright young men in television who p.obably do not own a suit and frequently do not wear a tie. One talented young director who used to work with me felt so stubborn about this that he wouldn't even wear a tie to his own wedding. And when the time for his promotion Board came I knew he'd behave in the same way and prejudice his chance of success with the more staid and senior members of the Board. I lent him my spare tie and firmly instructed him to wear it on the day. He did. To my horror, and the obvious irritation of my senior colleagues on the Board, the next three candidates all turned up wearing the same tie, my tie. The first man got the job. I've often wondered: had he been the second or third to wear my tie, would they have turned him down?

Esther was boarded once when she was a researcher in the Current Affairs Group and was trying to gain promotion to the job of junior director. She found it a hideous experience – nothing she said seemed to please the Board. 'I really felt as if I was standing there naked while they pointed out to each other all my physical failings,' she told her friends afterwards.

After half an hour of being finely minced they asked her if she had any questions for them. 'No,' she said. 'I'd just like to apologize to you all for wasting your time.'

Suddenly her interrogators turned into embarrassed, throat-clearing men who shuffled their papers and said 'Not at all, not at all,' 'Nice to meet you,' and so on. Jeremy Isaacs, who is now the Chief Executive of television's fourth channel, was editor of 'Panorama' at the time and on that Board. He bumped into Esther in the BBC reception area afterwards. 'Ludicrous exercise, Boards,' he said. 'Nothing to do with journalism, nothing to do with show business – just a terrible hangover from the Civil Service.'

The kind of person who sails through such Boards is like the producer who once worked with Esther. He was the prototype bullshitter. He leapt from one plum job to another, always being found out after about three months in each but always being promoted onwards. He could bluff his way into any conversation with tremendously impressive expertise. Once, he'd just been for a Board when she met him in the canteen.

She was, at that time, a radio studio manager and he was holding forth, as he had at the Board, about how incompetent, clumsy and stupid all studio managers are. She drank her coffee.

'Studio managers never understand the concept of acoustic silence,' he said.

'Pardon?' she said.

'That wonderful silence when all your hear is the acoustics of the room,' he said. 'One could do a whole play with the sound of someone breathing in a room.'

It was obvious that he had just been spouting that kind of garbage at his appointments Board. What's more it got him the job. And what's more a record company later brought out a record of total silence to prove him right.

Sometimes in order to 'get on' you have, first, to 'get out'. After two and a half years as a studio manager Esther resigned, bruised and defiant. Her pride cost her three months' unemployment until a wonderful BBC boss lady, Mrs Joanna Spicer, famous and unfortunately unique in her area, gave her a job as a clerk in the Programme Planning department. By that time Esther was grateful for any kind of job. Three days after she arrived in Planning and was put to work in the section dealing with Eurovision her boss went down with pneumonia. That left Esther in charge. 'I was terrific,' she remembers. In the BBC's Planning department they remember it too.

Esther had all the files sorted out in double quick time and as soon as a cable arrived asking for lines to be booked, or ordering time on the satellite, she popped it at once into its appropriate file. What no one had told her was that it was her job actually to make the booking before she filed the cable.

Slowly, international broadcasting ground to a standstill. But Esther was happy in her new task. She was still merrily filing away when, one morning, the elegant Mrs Spicer blew through the office door at some speed to inquire why a fistful of irate telegrams had arrived on her desk from producers whose programmes had never made the air. Esther smiled with a clear conscience. It wasn't her fault – and she could prove it. She led Mrs Spicer to the perfect files: filed but not acted on. The truth dawned on both of them. Mrs Spicer, a gentle impeccably mannered lady, started to talk about the possibility of finding Esther work somewhere else in the BBC, almost anywhere else.

As luck would have it, in the BBC Club at lunchtime (Ah, how many jobs have been lost and found in the BBC Club?) one of Esther's girlfriends mentioned the fact that Ned Sherrin was looking for a researcher. 'He's probably hell to work for,' said the friend. It was the job Esther most wanted in the world. Anyway, at that stage almost any job was likely to be the job Esther most wanted in the world. She ran back to her office and wrote asking to be interviewed.

Ned didn't hang around. He rang her the next morning and told her to come and see him at 8.30 the following morning. Ned used to be in the office at 7.00 a.m. and out again playing squash at 9.30. (He and David Frost both share a wonderful disregard for sleep – they only need three or four hours a night, which is, perhaps, why they seem to get through so many more careers and lives than the rest of us.)

Ned always does his homework. By the time Esther arrived in his office, mentally preparing the boring answers you need for Boards like: 'What you would put in "Panorama" tonight if you were producing it.' He had already discovered what he needed to know about this enthusiastic accident-prone girl from Programme Planning. He said 'Right, I can offer you a six-week contract.' For Esther it was like being offered the moon. Mrs Spicer let her go straight away, understandably enough when you consider what she'd already done to international broadcasting.

Ned Sherrin became deeply bored if he thought you knew your job and were not being stretched so every day he set Esther some impossible task, a stretching task. For one particular piece of research he asked her to read fifty-six volumes of Hansard in search of a single pointed quote, which he hoped existed.

Commander Courtney was an MP whom one of Ned's satirical friends had nominated as among the most boring in

Parliament. Was it true? Ned needed the proposition researched. And Esther discovered that she disagreed with the proposition. The more she read the more she realized that Commander Courtney had serious grounds for believing that the Russians and the Chinese were spying in large numbers using the diplomatic immunity of their cooks, gardeners and chauffeurs to disguise their real jobs as spies.

Again and again Commander Courtney asked questions about it in Parliament. You could, through the lines of Hansard, almost hear the sighs of boredom coming from the opposite benches. But that didn't make Commander Courtney and his persistent preoccupation boring in itself. Esther went back to Ned and said: 'I'm terribly sorry, I think he's probably slightly boring but that's only because he's convinced that there's a real threat in these embassies.'

Commander Courtney was not nominated in the satirical programme 'BBC-3' as the most boring MP in Parliament and fifty-six volumes of Hansard were returned to the library.

The story had an ironic twist, though. The KGB got the drop on Commander Courtney in the end. They produced compromising pictures of him with a Russian lady and used them in a smear campaign to try to drive him from public office and silence him. At the time the story broke Esther remembered one of the speeches she read in those volumes of Hansard. Commander Courtney had been reminiscing, in the Chamber, about a recent trade visit he'd made to Moscow. He told the Commons that, everywhere he went, he was followed by a particular security agent. In the end he became fed up with it and turned to the KGB man and said, 'Boris, I know you are simply following me to try and discover my secret weakness. Let me tell you what it is. I have a weakness for blondes.'

He told it as a joke. The moral seems to be, never tell jokes to Russians.

At the end of the series of 'BBC-3' Ned Sherrin left the BBC to work for Columbia Pictures as a producer. He had always been a reknowned talent spotter in the Corporation and he liked his discoveries to prosper. He did his best for Esther by writing her a flattering report. It was so good that the BBC, who had already extended her six-week contract to six months, promptly renewed it for another six months. Then the problem was what to do with her. If she had been a man it would have been easy. She had a fairly good degree and a kind report from Ned, so they could have made her a trainee producer – production assistant as they were called.

It was what she wanted, what she felt she was equipped to do. A lot of her male colleagues were doing just that, learning to direct film and research items for '24 Hours', the nightly news magazine. But she wasn't a man.

They sent her to talk to Dereck Amoore, the editor of '24 Hours'. He was brilliant, talented – and he had a lethal affection for an air gun that he carried with him most of the time. When he interviewed people he used to fire it at them or near them. Perhaps because he was short-sighted, thank God, he seldom hit them but the noise of the pellets whistling past job-applicants to ping on the aerosol spray balanced on the shelf behind their heads was believed to be the most severe form of distraction you could be exposed to in the whole of the BBC. He fired a shot or two at Esther.

'You've done very well,' he said. 'I've just the job for you – the photo library needs sorting.'

He led her to a long, narrow, sunless room, one wall lined with filing cabinets, their drawers so tightly packed with photographs they wouldn't shut. 'This is yours,' he said. 'Can you file them so that when researchers need a photograph urgently for a programme they can find what they need immediately.'

Esther is not too well brought up to swear. She smiled, nodded, waited until he'd gone and then ran into a friend's office and stamped round and round it shouting guttural monosyllables in old English. Swearing may be sinful and even unladylike but it makes you feel better.

She returned to her newly allocated priesthole and spent the next six months filing thirty-five thousand photographs. She even invented a new system by turning ordinary enve-lopes into photograph pouches, her tongue was thick with gum from sticking the flaps down. She managed, also, to borrow a secretary to help her. The secretary was a beauty queen from Zanzibar called Philomena. A lot of people suddenly started visiting Esther in her windowless room.

Finally came the wonderful day when Esther finished filing. Philomena typed a memo for her to Dereck Amoore. In it Esther explained that there was now an index card reference system. No more would there be different sets of photographs under P for Prince Philip and D for Duke of Edinburgh and Q for Queen's Husband – from now on there would be one envelope and all the other headings would be contained in the cross-reference system. But, said Esther in the memo, unless someone was asked to maintain the library, and its new system, the researchers running in and out, grabbing their photos and then shoving them back anywhere would destroy the system in a couple of weeks.

Dereck Amoore read the memo and called Esther to his office. 'I've read your comments and I agree with them,' he said. 'You're elected.' And he gestured with his air gun.

Esther left, rushed into the nearest office and did her war dance again. This time it was overheard by Tony Whitby, the assistant editor of '24 Hours' and later to become one of the best controllers Radio 4 has ever had. He listened to her old English and asked what was wrong. She told him. He winked at her and left the room.

In the meantime Dereck Amoore had asked Esther to tackle the filing cabinets immediately outside his own office and she went back to work on them. Amoore whiled away the time by firing pellets at an aerosol balanced on top of them. Esther was too far gone to care – one more minute and she was going to shy the aerosol back at him and tell him where to put his job. Resigning was getting to be a habit, the dole started to loom in her future once more.

Then Tony Whitby wandered by and gave a start of simulated surprise to see her. He said to Dereck, 'Is Esther still filing? I thought she'd finished.' Dereck said, 'She wrote me a memo saying someone ought to look after the photos permanently, so I told her she's elected.' Tony said, 'Don't you think she's a little expensive for the job?'

This struck Dereck as a new thought. Tony added, 'We've got one or two clerks on the programme who could include the library in their work without much trouble.' Dereck said, 'If you think that's more suitable, but what do we do with Esther?' Tony said, 'She's being paid as a researcher, I'll find something for her to research.'

He was as good as his word. While she was working for him he made her write scripts and songs and set up films and studio items. We all remember him with gratitude. He died tragically young. And, if it wasn't for him, Esther has no doubt she would still be filing photographs somewhere in a cell in Lime Grove.

So, how do the bosses themselves get on, climb from mini-boss to maxi-boss, from Big Chief to Biggest Chief? A finely honed survival sense is the main attribute.

Many bosses have an intuitive sonar system for trouble. They hear the 'ping' of its career-threatening approach from miles away. And then it's not for them the destroyer spirit of convoy escort captains hunting down submarines. Oh no, they go on a trip; at once, far away, for a long time, for very good reasons – preferably to China, or anywhere else where communication is difficult and from which they can return with the 'Now what has everybody been up to in my absence?' defence.

If the sonar 'ping' is too close to allow escape then the boss may have to come out in his true protective colours. I was once instructed by a senior BBC executive, when I was editor of 'Man Alive': 'I don't care how boring the programme is, as long as it doesn't cause any trouble.'

On that occasion I did a 'second take' but his face revealed nothing. He clearly meant it. Whatever happened he was going to get on.

In the BBC some bosses have polished a trick inherited from the smoother ranks of senior civil servants. It doesn't have a name but it could be called 'reversing the memo' and it's designed to re-write internal history in such a way that no hint of failure, hesitation, or wrong shall ever appear on the record attached to the boss's name. It works like this. A junior, a producer, programme editor or departmental head, writes a memo to one of his bosses complaining of an injustice to his staff or department, drawing attention to a planning error or a costly mistake. He may write sharply, or calmly, but the effect of the memo is the same. There, on the record, is evidence that the boss is flawed.

The same men who have a sonar detector system for career-shaking troubles ahead also have instant reflexes to deal with this sort of attack. They draw a line with an arrowhead at each end between their name at the top and your name at the bottom – reversing the memo back to you. Then they add a scribbled comment such as 'point taken', or 'don't get your dander up', or 'thanks, let's talk'. ('Talk' does not stay on the file and conversations are not carbon copied to the mightiest bosses, as some memos are.)

It means there is no longer any record of a mistake except, that is, on the files of the junior who is raising the issue. But once he has received the emasculating 'reversed memo' treatment, then his career card is 'marked', whether he knows it or not. He is most unlikely to 'get on'.

I never minded trouble if it was about an important issue, or to protect some journalistic principle but I was slightly indignant about one occasion which I provoked, quite accidentally.

We had planned an uncontroversial, entertaining public affairs programme about the future of the British film industry. Of course, the debate would be vigorous, the argument incisive, but it also contained feature film clips, always top box office appeal on television. I relaxed. It wasn't going to be a difficult week, rather an enjoyable one.

We started with the marvellous opening scene from *The Sound of Music* with Julie Andrews dancing through the Alpine meadows singing, to the helicopter above, that the hills were alive with the sound of box office takings. This was followed, on the television screen, by me earnestly explaining that films that didn't make the same tremendous profits as *The Sound of*

Music were, these days, in trouble – even if they had great artistic merit. Box office success now dominated film making – artistic achievement won praise but not the cash to keep going. There were a number of examples.

'Like this scene,' I proclaimed in genuine innocence, to the unseen millions of family viewers out there in the darkness. And we rolled on to the screen an excerpt from D. H. Lawrence's *Women in Love* in which Oliver Reed appears to be struggling hard with the more than willing Glenda Jackson to undo her suspender belt with his teeth, while they both rolled about in a rather muddy cornfield.

We followed with more film extracts and much vigorous debate from producers, union leaders and film critics. Unknown to us in the studio, the BBC switchboard was jammed with calls.

Viewers who had kept the children up late, and even brought granny down from upstairs to watch Julie Andrews, had been caught unawares and staggered, scandalized, to the phone to protest. How dare we? How could we? Why did we? 'Shocked of Cheltenham' and 'Disgusted of Tunbridge Wells' rose up in their scores. A future Labour Party Prime Minister telephoned to add his personal protest. He had been watching with his grandchildren and he didn't say: 'Just call me Jim.'

I had, quite literally, overlooked the fact that we were broadcasting X-certificate film material at eight o'clock in the evening, to the delight of many youngsters and the shock of nearly all their parents. An accident was the true reason – but it was not a good enough excuse.

Huw Wheldon, the Managing Director of BBC Television, sent for me to give what he declared in advance was to be 'the rocketing of my life' (and remember we both knew that he had to do very well indeed to beat some of the earlier ones I'd received at lower levels). I kept on smiling, couldn't stop.

'I really didn't realize what Oliver Reed was up to,' I said.

'What else could he have been doing?' Huw roared at me.

'Mending the road?' I suggested. That just made it worse.

But I couldn't get of my mind all those family groups gazing with pleasure at the virginal Miss Andrews, and then being confronted with the muddy lust of Oliver Reed's passion in a cornfield ... I like to think that Huw Wheldon was also amused. But he managed to keep his face straight, which is why he was a very good managing director.

My punishment? What else would you expect in the BBC - I had to write out lines, or rather I had to answer personally every complaint registered in the Duty Log. I wasn't chuckling by the time I reached the end of the list.

If it seems that getting on in television is more about not doing things than doing things, then I'm afraid that is one of the truer, and perhaps one of the sadder, facts of television life. People who leap to a challenge tend to trip up – and it is the people who don't trip who progress to the top. They may not exactly be plodders but their primary concern is, nevertheless, to place one foot carefully in front of the other on their personal career path. Advice on how to succeed usually amounts to a list of 'don'ts' rather than 'dos'.

For instance, don't use foul language on television. It may get you talked about but it won't get you promoted. You didn't see the Governors of the BBC rushing to offer Ken Tynan an executive position after he'd used what is usually thought of as the ultimate four-letter word in the middle of an interview with Robert Robinson on the satire programme 'BBC-3'. The paradox is that 'rude' programmes don't just attract complaints and rows with the bosses – they also attract viewers.

Esther was there at the time, in the control room. Tynan was being interviewed about changes in the theatre, and censorship, and discussing what was becoming acceptable and what boundaries had still to be pushed back as far as theatrical audiences were concerned.

Quite naturally, but also quite shockingly, Tynan chose to illustrate his point by saying that he thought it wouldn't be long before the ultimate word, and he paused and spoke it – 'fuck' – was commonly heard in certain productions. There was a long silence in the studio and the sound of the word seemed to echo. Robert Robinson stiffened rather like a man receiving 24,000 volts through his left heel but, courageous fellow that he really is, pressed on without betraying on his face the turmoil that had instantly entered his mind. Should he object? Should he draw attention to it? Should he comment disparagingly? But, by the time you've considered all these alternatives, it's already too late.

In the control room there was a stillness of the kind that is caused by a number of people all holding their breath together. The vision mixer continued to punch up the right camera and everybody else studiously went on with their jobs. Ned Sherrin, urbane and unflappable, in charge of it all, turned right round in his swivel chair to address the rest of the production team behind him: 'I suppose that's some kind of first,' he murmured, and returned to supervising the transmission. It certainly was.

The papers the next day were divided between those like the *Guardian*, which felt able to tell its readers exactly what word it was that the BBC transmitted to cause such shock (the phones were jammed with complaining viewers) and those which used bigger and blacker headlines to report the story but referred only to 'a four-letter word' or 'that word'. And Sherrin, unflustered, asked Esther to get him the originals of the many cartoons that appeared in the press.

'BBC-3' was a live programme and, therefore, the transmission which caused offence could not have been predicted or avoided. But that doesn't stop the powers that be from scowling generally in the direction of the offending programme and its team, on the grounds that one should somehow be skilful enough to avoid such accidents. And invitations to Kenneth Tynan to appear on television were few and far between after that. But the audience doubled, from four to eight million viewers, in one week.

These days, in television plays and documentaries, one can hear almost as a matter of course, a whole range of language likely to offend one's mother but nevertheless commonly heard in everyday circumstances. Perhaps one of the problems is that behind the scenes in television, as in journalism, publishing and the theatre, quite a lot of strong and unimaginative language is casually used, almost as a matter of course. It is, therefore, not surprising that some of it creeps past our inhibitions, and on to the air.

I've always prided myself on not giving this kind of offence while broadcasting and, indeed, in the days when I was a heavy smoker, not being seen to smoke on the air because of the harmful effects it might have on impressionable people. But into the lives of all who have pride, there is bound to come the fall.

I still get the shivers when I remember mine.

For some years in the early sixties I spent every Saturday night taking part in a regional current affairs programme called at first 'ABC at Large'. It was produced with verve and vigour on a small budget by Tom Brennand and Roy Bottomley, the two men who now mastermind 'This Is Your Life'.

Broadcasting to a soporific nation usually at about 11.30 at night we used to tackle meaningful issues in two or three minutes – and deeply philosophical ones in four or five.

With a song, a row, a clip of film and a few stills we would race through twenty-six minutes of air time every week.

One week they decided that the great issue to put before the viewers of the North and Midlands (the programme wasn't seen on the whole ITV network) was 'The price of a night out?'. I was chosen to present the item.

I arrived in Manchester on that Saturday morning, to be greeted by a minicab containing a luscious-looking blonde model in an evening dress and a secretary clutching a bunch of flowers and a box of chocolates, which were to be my 'props'.

We roared off in the direction of a newly opened nightclub in the Manchester suburbs as the secretary explained that the programme was to start with an outside broadcast directly from the nightclub with me explaining that I was conducting a consumer test on the cost of a typical night out. I would explain further that I had bought the lovely blonde a bunch of flowers and a box of chocolates and, at intervals during the programme, the viewers would return to the nightclub so that I could report to them how much our dinner had cost, what price the wine was, whether we'd spent any money at the gambling tables and what was the average tip to leave at the cloakroom. An 'in-depth' item.

In the nightclub, when we got there with some hours to go before the broadcast, all was chaos. The blonde settled happily in a corner with a woman's magazine, having been restrained from eating the prop chocolates before we went on the air, and I went in search of the stage manager. He is a vital technician on an outside broadcast unit, responsible for organizing and cueing what happens in front of camera, receiving his instructions from the mobile control room directly into earphones on his head. He is the only real link between a reporter and the director. Alarm bells should have sounded when I found him at the bar, comfortably at the bar, obviously having been there for some little time. But he was reassuring. He pointed out which camera I was to address, where I was to sit and the other locations, from the gaming room to the cloakroom, that we would move to in the course of this little soap opera.

Gradually the club filled up, cameramen and lighting technicians took their places, a sound man 'wired' me with a microphone, the owner of the club took me on one side and offered me a roll of fivers thick enough to choke a horse if I would mention the name of his club and its address several times.

Conscious of two things, my journalistic probity and the fact that every word he was whispering to me was undoubtedly being picked up on the microphone and broadcast to the mobile control van outside, I turned him down with what I hope was pleasant dignity.

We were due on the air at ten past eleven. At five past I began to worry about the absence of the stage manager. By then he should have been 'plugged in' to the camera facing me, giving me countdown timings to our live on-air cue. He couldn't be found.

With two minutes to go he appeared sleepily from one of

the back rooms with his headphones on but with the connecting lead coiled up in his hand as he ambled towards the bar. 'Oh God,' I thought. My blonde companion remained unmoved, practising her smile and fingering the box of chocolates, which she'd been promised she could open as soon as I'd mentioned them on the air. About three hundred people in the nightclub were gazing with interest at what they expected to be a kind of technical cabaret. Conversation had stopped, the club was hushed.

I called to the stage manager: 'Come on old boy, shouldn't you be over here now?'

He waved at me: 'Thash all right, losch of time.' He wasn't just drunk – he was paralytic. It was astonishing that he was still standing.

Forgetting the people in the club, forgetting everything else, I stood up behind the table, pointed a finger at him and roared at the top of my voice: 'Get your fucking finger out!'

Even as I uttered the words I noticed the red light come on the camera in front of me. We were 'live' on the air.

The cameraman, peering round his machine, was making mouthing gestures and waving frantically at me to sit down. I got the message. I sat down and stammered the prepared introduction: 'Tonight we're taking a look at the price of a night out. I've bought flowers and chocolates for this lovely lady here. There'll be dinner and perhaps even gambling to follow. But how much is it going to cost? And can I afford it? We'll be back later.'

I heard, faintly from the cameraman's headphones, the sound of the opening music which was being broadcast from the studio in Manchester. I knew there were three or four minutes before they were due to come back to the nightclub. I grabbed the cameraman's headphones and pulled down the switch which enabled me to talk to the director in the mobile control room. 'What shall I do? Shall I apologize? Explain? Or ignore? Will you ask the main studio control room?'

Seconds later he gave me the answer: 'Press on as though it hadn't happened.' And then he relaxed his professional manner to add: 'Cor, Des, that's one for the book,'

Miserably I wandered back to my table, my career in ruins. The lovely blonde was half-way through the chocolates and an ashen-faced stage manager, who was now plugged in to the camera, was rubbing his face with a handkerchief soaked in cold water and clearly sobering up very fast indeed.

We staggered through the programme. We pretended to eat dinner, gambled a little, discussed the price of wine, tipped the cloakroom lady and added up the bill for the viewers. At last we came off the air. I tore outside to the control van. On the phone to Roy Bottomley, in the studio in Manchester, I asked with a sinking heart: 'Were there many phone calls about it?'

'About fifty or sixty so far and more coming in,' he told me.

My fate was sealed. 'Oh God, it's really bad isn't it?' I said. 'What sort of things did they say?' Mentally I was wondering if I could re-establish a career in newspapers or magazines, and vowing, also, to see that the stage manager not only didn't live past midnight but that when he died he did so at my hands.

Roy Bottomley replied: 'Well, of the calls we've had so far, fifty-nine of them have congratulated us on the new title of the programme – and one person rang asking for the phone number of the blonde at your table.'

And that's the way it remained. I was saved. We never did re-name the programme, although by then the Duke of Edinburgh had made the words 'get your finger out' a universally acceptable phrase; but not with the adjective I had added to it on the air. I received a comprehensive apology from the stage manager but it still lacked the one assurance that I would have needed before working with him again. He didn't announce that he had become teetotal.

3 The Bosses

The mark of a true boss is that he is the kind of person that nobody can ever imagine being anything other than a boss, recognizable immediately as the authority figure in the lives of others. In television, bosses come in all shapes and sizes, sometimes even in apparently democratic form. They don't necessarily need cigars or chauffeurs to convey their rank. There is usually just something 'big' about their presence.

I never worked directly for Lew Grade but he, among all the bosses, has always been my idea of the archetypal television mogul. It isn't just the enormous cigar, jutting ahead like the bowsprit of a clipper ship. There is, too, a manner about him, not unlike a square-rigged sailing ship. He sails through rooms and probably through life. There are many stories told about him.

In the early days of commercial television in this country, shortly after we had all begun to recover from our delight and wonderment at the commercial jingles and our fascination with the intrigues of 'Coronation Street' and 'Jim's Inn', Lew Grade was beginning his long career from boss to superboss. He had not, at that time, become Lord or even Sir but it was obvious to everybody that it was only a matter of time.

The voices of critics had been raised suggesting that the new commercial channel was long on entertainment and short on culture. The response of ITV was dramatic. They would produce 'Hamlet', a full version – hours of Shakespeare; culture, with a capital K.

The schedules were cleared, the commercial breaks pushed aside and the screens of Independent Television filled with the passions and intrigues of Elsinore. It was a good production too, well acted, well directed, gripping.

In the last scene of the last act, as usual, the stage gradually became crowded with corpses as the sword fights brought the tragedy to its close.

But in the TV version, just before the final moment, the screen shimmered and dissolved – into a line of dancing oranges with little mouths obscenely opening and closing. As they high-kicked across the screen, squeaky dubbed-on voices chorused: 'Kia-ora, Kia-ora, the squash that's fit to drink,' and so on . . .

In Television House, Kingsway there was a young, brand new producer on duty in the Presentation Control Room. He had the responsibility for co-ordinating the transmission of 'Hamlet' to all fifteen of the ITV network regions. The production secretary passed him the phone with the blood-chilling words: 'It's Mr Lew Grade, he wants to talk to you.'

'Sir.'

'What happened? What the devil happened?' barked the boss who had specially cleared an evening's schedules in order to present Shakespeare unadorned – only to see his plan shattered by a commercial; effectively inflicting on the nation 'Hamlet interruptus'.

Moments like this produce ice in the brain, reflexes take over. 'Oh Sir,' said the young producer. 'They all died in the end . . .'

Bosses like toys. They also like their toys to be bigger and better than other television bosses'. Office curtains that open and close at the touch of a switch, golfball typewriters for the secretary in the outer office, the latest intercom. And phones, push button, memory holding, presidential hotline, coloured phones; but particularly phones in cars.

Once, when I visited Granada Television in Manchester, I was hospitably met at the airport by a chauffeur-driven car. As we cruised through the outer suburbs of Manchester a warbling sounded from somewhere in the upholstery of the front passenger seat.

'It's the phone for you, sir,' said the chauffeur. Deeply impressed, I searched for it, found it and picked it up.

A girl's voice said: 'Welcome to "Granadaland", Mr Wilcox. You should be with us in twenty minutes, is there anything you would like arranged to wait for you?'

I shook my head, struck dumb by this service from a super-boss. Unfortunately head shakes don't communicate at all well by phone and to my relief I heard the smoothness of the lady's professional manner slip a little as she said: 'Are you there? Has it broken again?' I reassured her and felt better. The world was human after all and machines were not infallible.

The Managing Director of BBC Radio, Aubrey Singer, had a truly magic car telephone installed when he reached his eminent position. We went to lunch together and on the way back he demonstrated it for me. A tiny flashing red light scurried up and down a dial, like a rabbit trying to escape a stoat, searching for a bolt hole in the shape of an available radio frequency. When it finally discovered it, the operator asked for the number. Aubrey, a man with ironmongery to hand but at a loss for a cause, telephoned his secretary to let her know that he would have lemon tea that afternoon, as he had every afternoon for fifteen years.

Being a generous man, a good friend and a boss to the manner born, he climbed out of the car at Broadcasting House saying: 'Take the car on, it'll be quicker for you.' (I was going back to Shepherd's Bush.) Then he added what must, for him, have been the most generous of all invitations: 'Feel free to use the phone.' He waved and was swallowed by the building.

Why not? Chauffeured in comfort at sixty miles an hour

along the Westway I decided to use the phone. I didn't need to, but I wanted to. Unimaginatively, I telephoned my own secretary, Lorna, and ordered lemon tea for my return in a few minutes. 'I can't hear you properly. It's a very bad line. Where are you?' she bellowed.

'I'm speaking on a telephone from the back of Aubrey Singer's car,' I pointed out.

'I still can't hear you properly. Can you go to another telephone box?'

Limply I gave up and put the phone down. To my horror it broke into three separate pieces and fell on the carpet at my feet. The chauffeur, a calm, experienced man, displayed real emotion: 'Oh Gawd, Mr Singer was ever so fond of that.' My career may never have truly recovered from that day.

Aubrey Singer is, however, a rare kind of boss. He likes a joke. He also likes travelling and, for weeks on end, will endure aeroplane food, hotel living and foreign climates. More than anybody, he was responsible for rediscovering China for the BBC. On one of his early exploration trips, he agreed to visit Ulan Bator, the capital city of Outer Mongolia, for me. I wanted 'Man Alive' to make a film about our ambassador in this remote, largely tented, city and Aubrey generously offered to save me the trouble of having to discover its exotic delights personally.

In the only hotel, he met and became friendly with two members of the Foreign Office. They were leaving to return home before him and agreed to leave behind a particularly valuable commodity, a roll of toilet paper, difficult to get in Outer Mongolia.

It was outside Aubrey's door the next morning. Gratefully he placed it in his bathroom. Some time later he had occasion to look at it more closely. Carefully written in ballpoint on every single sheet was a communique from the Foreign Office to the Corporation: 'Up the arse of the BBC'.

David Attenborough, one of the best bosses I've ever worked for, never set out to be a boss, was brilliant at it and – in the end – turned his back on it to return to his first love, natural history film making round the world.

He was responsible for persuading me to leave commercial television and join the BBC in 1965 when he had just been appointed Controller of the brand new BBC-2. He got his job out of the blue. He was packing portable canoes, haversacks, tents and supplies on the top of a landrover outside his Richmond home, in preparation for another 'Zoo Quest', when the phone call came from the BBC Television Centre asking him if he'd stop being a documentary producer and start being a boss, a big boss.

Although in the end he grew weary of the demands placed on his time – 'It's like being a dentist, my damned diary is divided into fifteen-minute segments now,' he told me once – he never lost his sense of humour when it came to observing the rest of the human race; particularly his own species, BBC bosses.

In his new sixth-floor office at the Television Centre – very different from the tent in Africa he might have been occupying – he discovered that he could be supplied with bottles of Malvern water from the executive kitchen just across the corridor. Each day a fresh bottle of Malvern water and a glass sat on their own piece of white blotting paper, on the corner of his desk. Not for him the interminable cups of heart-stimulating, gut-rotting, coffee or the fortifying sherry which taken too early in the day can blur television judgement at executive level.

To his delight, within six weeks, the desks of other controllers of equal rank, and several ambitious executives of slightly junior rank, had all sprouted bottles of Malvern water ...

'I didn't really like the stuff very much but I didn't want to lose touch with the kind of observations that I most enjoyed making when I was studying the aggressive and imitative behaviour patterns of certain animals. I had, long before, decided that there was an interesting academic paper to be written entitled: "Some Observations on the Rituals Connected with Seating Patterns in BBC Committees" and I thought it might be fun to see just how long it was before this sharp-beaked tribe, called BBC bosses, felt disturbed by the introduction of a new environmental element to a point where, defensively, they had to respond in the same manner.

'If that sounds patronizing then it wasn't how I felt. It was just a way of clinging to my sense of sanity in those new conditions,' he told me.

Most bosses in any industry develop eccentricities and in television there is a whole range of eccentricities which are almost a cultivated part of the media boss persona.

Bill Cotton wears his father's shoes and is proud to tell you so. Indeed, sitting beneath a cartoon of Billy Cotton Sr, he'll add: 'That's all he left me, that and a wristwatch.'

But Alasdair Milne, the Managing Director of BBC Television, tends to slip his shoes off whenever he's sitting down. He'll then come out from behind his desk in order to start marching about his room to make a point more strongly, in his socks.

Unfortunately, I've always had the same unconscious habit. Esther and I are often last out of the cinema because I'm on my hands and knees among the ice cream cartons and cigarette ends groping for my shoes.

On one occasion, in Alasdair Milne's office, we were having an argument. The more stubbornly I made my points the more firmly he rejected them. In the end justice prevailed, as it always does in organizations like the BBC. 'I'm the Managing Director. We'll do it my way.'

The discussion was over, it was time to leave, smartly. Then I discovered I was in my socks. I started to feel around with my feet for my shoes. To my relief, I found them quickly. I stood up, slipping my heels home and made one of those idiotically dignified exits, of the sort common to junior bosses who've just been overruled by senior bosses, on an end line like: 'Well, we'll just have to agree to disagree.' I left the office, stiff with dignity.

In the corridor outside I had only taken two steps before

a sharp pinching sensation made me realize I was wearing one of the Managing Director's shoes and one of my own. It spoils dignified exits when you have to return wearing a shoe and a sock and clutching one of your boss's shoes to ask him to step out of one of your own.

Actually, he made the exchange quite absent-mindedly, murmuring, 'I always thought you had smaller feet than me.'

Mind you, even managing directors have their bosses. In ITV companies it's the Board of the Independent Broadcasting Authority and the Chairman; and in the BBC the board of Governors and their Chairman. Both Chairmen are appointed by the Prime Minister, the Boards are chosen by the Home Office. The Governors of the BBC have for some years past been extending their authority, frustrated in the past by their separation from the executive decision making of the BBC. Nowadays they make the most senior appointments and so, increasingly, the top men of the BBC are chosen not by their professional colleagues but by twelve ladies and gentlemen who may know little about broadcasting. They are wise enough in their own worlds, which range from the Chair of Poetry at Oxford to trade union office or a Foreign Office pension. They work hard and try to protect the best interests of the BBC but they must also represent the best interests of the public. And that is sometimes an impossible compromise. Their main purpose then becomes stopping the BBC from getting into trouble.

As a result maverick programme makers, executives who talk too much, or appear in the newspapers, are obviously 'bounders', not to be trusted with 'Auntie' because they're bound to get her into trouble. It means that some talented men in the BBC will never hold high office. It means, also, that most of the appointments are made from the ranks of those who have never themselves made waves.

And yet sometimes mavericks are responsible for the most moving moments in television. When the Russian tanks rolled into Czechoslovakia, the television programme makers took to the streets and showed the world the truth – the Czecho-slovakian people pleading with the invading soldiers.

No one who saw those tragic pictures can forget them – or the courage of the programme makers who were prepared to risk everything to tell the truth. They made waves all right.

There are similar testing situations closer to home, such as Northern Ireland and Watergate. If we are to maintain the courage of our own television programme makers, then television must have bosses who are prepared to take a stand – even to make waves – in the cause of truth.

4 The studio

The heart of any television organization is the television studio itself. Film locations are glamorous, sometimes even romantic; outside broadcasts are urgent and dramatic; feature films and American soap operas pay the rent by bringing in the viewers but, at the the centre of it all, is the studio.

It's in studios that television magic is created. Basically they are cavernous, windowless, aircraft hangers with hundreds of lights suspended from above, and the complicated 'space-age' control rooms set high in the walls. A studio is, in bald terms, no more than a place for cameras, microphones, actors and performers to produce together television for the screen. But there's more to it than that.

Studios become transformed with scenery, with props, with Persian carpets painted with great skill on the black tiled floor. During a few hours at night – and the most elaborate sets and effects usually are created by a night shift – the living rooms of 'The Forsyte Saga', the headquarters of Newtown Police, the royal chambers of Henry VIII will be brought to life by carpenters, painters and designers.

It's all false, of course. The panelling and fireplaces are made not from oak and stone but plaster and ply; the elegant gardens and distant parklands are brought into being with plastic shrubs or rented greenery in pots which are hidden underneath acres of nylon grass. The props are real though, rented from antique shops, or borrowed from collectors, to add authenticity to a set.

And the costumes are created after weeks of careful research to reflect exactly the period and style needed. They may look historically authentic but in order to work well on television they are often made of surprising junk. Bottle tops and cheap beads look better on camera than doubloons and diamonds. Rubberized material will serve better than priceless silk. All part of the magic.

Light Entertainment sets, with staircases stretching to infinity and abstract arrangements of wire, perspex and glitter will bring the days of the great Broadway musicals into our sitting rooms. It all needs lighting to bring it properly alive and some of the lighting engineers in television studios are able to use their equipment the way an artist conveys atmosphere and colour with a paintbrush.

The thing that surprises visitors to studios is that it all seems to be in miniature. Studio audiences can look at a whole row of tiny rooms which, because of lighting and the kind of lenses used, the viewer will think are huge.

The tragedy, in a way, of this magical pantomime effect is the insubstantial nature of it all. Hours after a play or programme is finished, palaces are torn down, courtrooms demolished, stately homes flattened – all to make way for a new fantasy, tomorrow's creation. Economically it is cheaper to destroy sets than to pay for the storage space against the possibility they may be needed again.

There are snags too. Designers tend to fall for fashionable devices, all at the same time. Like all those damned plants. Michael Parkinson complains on the air about them on the set of his programme. And, on 'That's Life!', Cyril Fletcher sometimes appears to have an aspidistra growing out of his head. But without a studio in which to operate, programmes like 'That's Life!' couldn't exist.

Nobody knew it better than John Lloyd, the first producer of 'Braden's Week' and the man who discovered Esther

Rantzen in an 'on-screen' role. He was a dry, witty, totally lovable Welshman. He was small, bespectacled, balding, fierce in his passions about rugby and beer, and mild in his observations about everything important, like politics and the BBC. He never would join the staff of the BBC and always remained a freelance.

'It would be too hypocritical,' he used to tell us. 'I couldn't take their money as a staff man. Somehow I feel that it would mean I would have to stop laughing at them – and the only thing that makes the job half bearable is being able to laugh at them.'

He's dead now, tragically early, and the world is a poorer place and this book is named in memory of one of his wry television observations in the hope that he might have approved of the stories in it.

Like all talented writers he was always just about to write the definitive novel. It never became the completed novel because he always started by writing the reviews first. Also, he could never find a thriller plot to fit either of his two titles, both of which derived, he said, from the ludicrous jargon which those of us who work in television take for granted but which makes visitors from the outside world anxious to hurry back to it.

I was with him in the studio control room when he discovered the first title. He wasn't paying much attention to the way Esther Rantzen, fellow reporter John Pitman and actors Chris Munds and Hilary Pritchard were, with Bernie Braden, bringing his script to life during rehearsal. He'd persuaded the technical manager to plug in the rugger match on one of the monitors and he had, as usual, persuaded me to bet £2 that Wales would lose.

He sat there like a greedy sparrow in anticipation of a certain worm, his bright eyes gleeful with the thought of victory and profit, when he cocked his head to one side, as though hearing a distant Indian war cry.

The studio director was having trouble with a two-line sketch which depended on Hilary Pritchard pretending to be on a diet, and cheating. The exchange was taking place at full shout on the studio floor between the floor manager and his assistant. The floor manager was bellowing in order to be heard through the microphone by the director upstairs. It went as follows: 'Is the chocolate biscuit dead?'

'Yes.'

'Right, kill the chocolate biscuit.'

What they meant was that the problem of lighting and photographing the chocolate biscuit would take too long – cake would have to do instead. It made perfect sense to everybody in the studio.

It also made perfect nonsense to the finely tuned, appreciative ear of John Lloyd. He explained to me that it was, for him, the ideal title for a thriller. 'Together with a picture of a naked woman, how can it fail?' He also told me the story of his other favourite title.

A colleague of his was making a short film for the original 'Tonight' programme in a crematorium. The last sombre moments of the ceremony had just been reached when, as always seems to happen on such occasions, the cameraman whispered that he'd run out of film.

John's friend, absorbed totally in his artistic mission, rushed down the aisle, calling: 'Please could we have the coffin back?'

Both phrases, John decided, summed up the lunatic nature of the world in which we all earned our living. He wrote about it once in the *Listener* (I have paraphrased his words) and I never dreamed, as I laughed out loud while reading it, that the day would come when I would read his piece to an audience as part of the tributes to him in a memorial evening at the British Academy of Film and Television Arts. He was only thirty-seven when he died of cancer. Without people like him the business of television is like bread without yeast.

As I said, John Lloyd first put Esther Rantzen on the television screen. She and John Pitman were working as researchers on the first edition of 'Braden's Week' and John Lloyd was searching for a formula that would allow him to script the consumer material for more than one voice. After listening to an exchange in the office one afternoon (in which it was clear that young Rantzen believed the man under investigation to be the biggest crook since Nero and Pitman thought him a misunderstood citizen, with personal hang-ups that needed sympathy) he knew he had the formula: Braden the Solomon figure, and Esther and John the protagonists.

Esther's career on television had begun. Week after week she and John Pitman sat side by side under the lights eager and bright-eyed as a pair of puppies for sale in a pet shop window.

One Saturday during rehearsals a scene hand appeared behind them. 'Psst. Do you want to buy a wristwatch? I've got a lady's and a gent's, brand new, half price.' Pitman was interested enough to try one on. Rantzen was, as usual, broke. Studios are notorious places for 'fell-off-a-lorry' bargains so neither of them could have been in much doubt about the watches being 'hot'. Just how hot, they were soon to discover.

The next item to be rehearsed concerned a viewer's complaint that a well-known range of wristwatches advertised on television didn't live up to some of the claims made for them. Bernie Braden, introducing the item, strolled across the studio floor to a mock-up of a jeweller's counter with a green baize tray on top of it. He reached the counter and stretched out for the watches in the tray.

The tray was empty.

At the time, Esther was looking directly at the scene hand who had so recently tried to interest her in a bargain. She swears he didn't even blink as he gazed back at her. And she didn't have the nerve to say anything.

In the ensuing fuss the item was cut from the running order and the pressure of rehearsal closed round everybody again. After the programme was over a 'theft-or-lost' form was filled in by those responsible for the studio props, with the phrase 'unaccountably lost during production', so often used in studios.

I don't want to give the idea that television studios are places where you find common thieves. There's nothing common about the thieves in television studios, they're superb.

In the 1960s I was working as a reporter on 'This Week'

when a new system of egg production was introduced to this country – battery hen farming. The poor, inoffensive little red hens of our great animal-loving nation were no longer going to be allowed to scratch contentedly around the farmyard, laying eggs in nesting places known only to the farmer's wife.

The 'new order' consisted of a wire wall of cages, each a little bigger than the hen, in which the creatures were doomed to sit all their lives, their heads sticking out of one end for the regular refills of corn and water dispensed automatically into trays in front of their beaks. Their bums stuck out of the other end, above the metal slideway which would take, and roll away, the regularly produced eggs.

I don't know why I believe that the hen battery is a German invention but somehow I seem to remember that it was, although it may only be an association of ideas. Not unnaturally, its introduction as a British farming method caused uproar. And uproar was my job.

We persuaded the Ministry of Agriculture and Fisheries, who were anxious to explain and defend the new farming innovation as being not anything like as cruel as its accusers thought, to bring a hen battery to Television House, Kingsway; and a dozen hens and (just in case they wouldn't produce on cue) three dozen eggs – without the lion stamps.

The 'props' duly arrived and the studio director and I discovered that the machine that travelled up and down feeding and watering the hens made a very loud noise indeed, too loud for the studio. But not too loud for the scenery 'dock' just outside through the double doors of the studio. Good enough. That's where we would do the interview. A camera could be pushed through the doors, lighting could be arranged, Desmond and the man from the Ministry, plus the accusing chicken-lover, could conduct the discussion standing up in front of the hen battery while the feeding trough shunted backwards and forwards behind them and the little Rhode Island Reds peered beadily over the shoulders of the participants. We rehearsed, rearranged the lighting, placed the eggs where they would show best and the hens where they could be seen.

'This Week' was a live programme so we waited to one side of the studio floor for the remaining ten minutes until our on-air cue. On the air the hens clucked, the machine travelled backwards and forwards, one obliging bird even laid an egg in the middle of the item, the man from the Ministry defended valiantly and the hen-lover went for his ministerial jugular, condemning battery farming for ever with the appalling, but unforgettable, label 'Hen Belsens'.

After eleven minutes the item was over and the rest of the programme, a political interview between Brian Magee and a properly balanced stonewalling act of two politicians, continued. With my interviewees, I tiptoed out behind the camera for a drink in the 'Green Room'.

Barely ten minutes had gone by and the programme was still on the air when the man from the Ministry asked me to show him the way back to the studio so that, with his assistants, he could box up the hen battery, hens and eggs. As we got there the programme finished. The studio was crowded with men lowering lights and moving scenery.

In the scene dock the hen battery still stood in the glare of the spotlight. Empty.

Not a hen, not an egg, not even a feather to show. The programme had been off the air less than thirty seconds. If anybody had touched a hen during the broadcast the clucking would have been heard. Nobody had left the studio or its immediate area. Pockets were emptied, jackets held open, dark corners of the studio explored. No eggs. No chickens. Nothing.

The man from the Ministry was almost weeping with frustration. Officials were called, investigations were promised, culprits would be found, punished. Recompense would be made.

The clearest memory of the whole incident, that I can never put out of my mind, is of the open-faced, trusting-eyed expressions of concern on the faces of all those scene hands. It was, for them, so obviously such a mystery and they would so liked to have seen it solved . . .

W. C. Fields is supposed to have said, 'Never work with

children or animals.' He was right. Animals in studios are notorious. Strong men go pale and start to shake when told they must either perform in the same programme with, or produce, animals – and animals means anything from a visiting flea circus to baby elephants. There can hardly be anybody who hasn't by now heard of, or seen in those comic 'Review of the Year' programmes, the occasion when the baby elephant visited the 'Blue Peter' studio.

Valerie Singleton, John Noakes and Peter Purves were the three presenters and the formidable, talented Biddy Baxter the producer. Her name is now synonymous with 'Blue Peter'. It was Biddy who decided that the normal method of restraining the baby elephant would look cruel to the young viewers, even if it wasn't. So the keeper's hooked stick which is normally used behind the elephant's ear was banished, and half a ton of skittish elephant flesh was fitted with a giant-sized, and gentle, dog collar and lead; comforting for the young viewers – and useless for restraining the young lady elephant.

'Live' on the air they introduced the elephant to the children remarking how much she ate and drank. To prove the point they gave her a bucket of water which she syphoned up in seconds. Only seconds after that, she proceeded to pass the water straight back to the studio floor. Valerie said, 'Ooops!', John Noakes said, 'Oh, we're having a slight penny down here!' The elephant then decorated her puddle with several large plops. The three presenters valiantly pressed on with the final minutes of the programme, telling the children what was in store and waving goodbye to the elephant as the hapless keeper attempted to lead her out of shot on the end of a thin piece of leather better suited to taking a peke for a walk.

The elephant dragged him first one way then the other. At one stage she paused again by John Noakes. 'Ooh, get off me foot,' he yelled. Finally she ambled off in an entirely new direction still dragging her unwilling keeper tottering behind her clutching the end of the useless lead. Tottering that is, until he reached the large puddle, at which point he skidded, his feet went up and he vanished from shot being towed on his back, through the puddle.

The presenters pressed on. 'That'll be all from us, we'll be back on Thursday,' said Valerie.

John Noakes, walking backwards as he waved to the young viewers started to say of the elephant 'There she goes right out of the studio ... oops, I've trodden in it,' and looked most unavuncular for a moment as the familiar trilling 'Blue Peter' signature tune began to sound and the scene faded.

Much to the credit of the 'Blue Peter' team, and those presenters who've since gone on to even greater achievements, they seem not to mind when in any catalogue of BBC disasters the recording of that desperate moment is replayed.

As far as I can find out, there is no recording of the time Huw Wheldon, then the presenter of a children's programme called 'All Your Own', met with a disaster a hundred times worse.

A schoolboy had been reported in the papers as the owner of two unusual pets which showed great friendship for each other – an eagle and a mouse. He was photographed with them and, naturally, invited by the 'All Your Own' production team to bring this exotic friendship to the studio.

The programme went on the air, the time came for the young viewer and his pets to be introduced. Huw Wheldon explained to the cameras and the television audience of young viewers why and how and what was about to happen.

'In a minute we will show you this remarkable friendship between two animals. You see,' he explained carefully, 'the mouse is normally the natural prey of the eagle. There's nothing cruel about this. It is, as I'm sure you all appreciate and learn at school, nature's way. We are, all of us, meat eaters. Among human beings some of us choose to be vegetarian but that isn't the sort of decision that you could expect from either the brain or the instincts of a beautiful hunting creature like the eagle ...'

And so he went on, ignoring the sound of some studio kerfuffle, behind him. The moment arrived. 'Now let's have a look,' he said and proceeded to walk towards the boy who stood with the eagle on a tall loggy birdstand.

But where was the mouse? The schoolboy was looking devastated, a floor manager just out of vision appeared distraught – and the eagle seemed very smug indeed.

The bird had, of course, (as Huw Wheldon would explain) 'succumbed to his deep primordial instincts'. In an attack of stage fright, he had eaten his friend, the mouse.

Somehow they got round it and somehow they got off the air, thankfully. Animals again.

An ordinary house fly once presented the most unflappable man on television, Patrick Moore, with an excruciating dilemma.

Patrick Moore is, of course, unique. Nobody speaks faster or dresses worse. His 'The Sky at Night' programme is one of the longest running television series on the air. I ought to know, it was for many years my responsibility – and I enjoyed it greatly. Indeed, I joined the distinguished ranks of those invited to contribute a foreword to the very successful annual book he writes at the end of each series.

If you tell him that he's proposing to get too many words into the short time available, you invite disaster. He will not cut words, but he will speak even more quickly. Standing like an animated grizzly bear in an Oxfam suit, he will scowl at the camera from beneath a gigantic pair of overhanging eyebrows and yell astronomical facts at a middle-of-the-night television audience at the speed of somebody attempting to machine gun viewers, rather than educate them. Rightly, he has always been popular.

Before one live programme, we once did tell him there were too many words – and he did speak faster. And then the fly arrived, an ordinary black house fly. It circled his head several times causing him to squint wildly. The viewers could not have missed it. It was a big fly and buzzed very loudly.

Patrick didn't slow down, didn't hesitate. Venus was wherever it was, Jupiter was doing its thing and the major constellations were remorselessly set on their astral courses. He drew breath to continue – and the fly went straight into his mouth.

There was a moment of magic stillness during which Patrick remained silent with his mouth open, quite evidently considering the awkward options ahead of him. What should he do? To spit would seem inelegant, unscientific. To wait any longer was not in his nature. There was almost time for those in the control room to take bets on the issue.

Patrick decided. He closed his mouth firmly. And swallowed.

He started speaking again, rapidly, firmly, authoritatively, as though nothing had happened. In the control room half the production team groaned and some, I have to confess, cheered. I believe money changed hands.

Esther not only never seems to learn about animals in 'That's Life!', she positively courts disaster.

A viewer had written to her complaining that some pellets called Scent Off, which were designed to deter dogs from peeing on lawns, didn't work. Not only that, the viewer's dog ate the pellets with relish and then went on to bless the lawn, the flowers, the paths and everything else in sight. Weaker people would have found some other consumer test for that programme – something comparatively safe, like parachutes not opening, or knives not cutting. Not Esther.

Ten dogs were organized by the production team for the day of the programme. They belonged to the team themselves, or relatives, or friends and they ranged from a Pekinese to a Great Dane. They included an affectionate Airedale who looked exactly like Fyfe Robertson and my favourite dog, the Welsh Collie belonging to Esther's producer, which used to display Everest levels of intelligence by lying down at my feet whenever I came into the room.

During rehearsal the dogs stood on leads each with their owner in front of a little pile of Scent Off pellets. They were invited to sniff or to ignore them. It was rather a dull performance.

I felt that the dogs were probably restrained by being on their leads and suggested that when the time came for the broadcast the owners should let them off the leads. 'But there'll be chaos,' said Esther.

'Oh no, surely not,' I replied. 'Anyway, it isn't a real consumer test as it is. It doesn't determine anything about the pellets' effectiveness.'

There are strict rules about animals in studios and our floor manager was preoccupied with other problems while this conversation went on. He would almost certainly, otherwise, have drawn our attention to the rules and told us the dogs were not allowed off their leads.

The audience arrived, 'That's Life!' began, the moment came and the owners were instructed, on the air, to let their dogs off the leads. A look of panic crossed the floor manager's face, too late. It was, of course, pandemonium.

The first thing all the dogs did was vanish into the audience causing squeaks, roars and yells as people tried to round them up and return them to the stage of the Television Theatre. The camera crew, entering into the spirit of things managed to follow some of the best action since the last FA Cup final. The dogs explored their way back to the stage. Esther began to wind up the item and move towards the end of the programme. But the audience were, by now, screeching with laughter and pointing. All the dogs were eating the Scent Off pellets as though they were chocolate drops and behind Esther the Airedale had decided to christen the potted ferns, beloved of all television set designers. He was starting an instant canine fashion. Cyril Fletcher's chair, all available greenery, and various microphone stands, came in for the raised leg treatment. My favourite Welsh Border Collie went for the throat of the amiable Great Dane. The Pekinese tried to bite the floor manager. Several cameramen nearly choked with laughter – and the programme over-ran its time by five minutes.

At BBC Television's weekly Programme Review Board, the important meeting where heads of departments discuss the programmes of the previous week and the viewing figures, I was taken to task by that veteran of variety, Bill Cotton, the Controller of BBC-1. Should I have let it happen? Could I have prevented it? It was obviously my administrative responsibility.

I suppose he was right but the next week two million more viewers tuned in to 'That's Life!' just in case it happened again. It never did.

Make-up, lipstick, powder, Sun Goddess No. 7, hair pieces – all are an essential concomitant of television studios. Unlike the film industry, where nearly all make-up artists are men, chauvinism works in reverse in television and the make-up artists are all women. And just as a man has no secrets from his valet, so do people in television manage to hide nothing from the make-up girls. Every production uses make-up, even the most unglamorous and undramatic current affairs interview usually needs a dab of powder before it is transmittable. Baldness shines, pinkness glows and neither looks good on the screen. Mind you, having such talented ladies in the building also has its advantages for the executives.

I remember once waiting with some interviewees for our make-up lady to arrive and when she did, apologizing in a fluster for being late, she explained that she had been cutting and blow-drying the hair of one of the channel controllers. His thick, silvery locks never looked the same again to me.

Make-up ladies are normally unshockable. There's very little they haven't seen or heard behind the polished images that appear on the television screen. But they were shocked, once, by the insensitive behaviour of an international singing star.

He arrived at the BBC to do a 'special' and spent a great deal of time in make-up ensuring that the casual hairstyle and the sun tan were perfect. He ignored repeated warnings from the call boy that the studio was waiting to record his number. Finally, the warnings were accompanied by threats from the director.

'But I gotta pee,' said the star, splendid in a duelling blouse and tight velvet trousers.

And he walked over to the hand basin in the corner – and, in front of them all, he peed. He must have sensed the shock he had caused because he turned his head to look at the make-up ladies and with a smile told them, 'You really oughta feel privileged to see it.'

They clearly weren't. I found it nearly impossible, watching him on the Michael Parkinson show the other night, to listen to his disarming conversation about himself and get that incident out of my mind.

The performers depend not only on make-up to look good but on autocue to sound good. On programmes like 'That's Life!', 'Man Alive', 'TV Eye' (which, when I worked on it in the days of stone age television, always seemed much better named 'This Week') the autocue is essential. It's the modern equivalent of Bob Hope's 'Cue Boards' or 'idiot cards'. The script is typed out and unrolled in front of the camera. These days this television prompter is so skilfully designed that, because of an arrangement of mirrors, the television presenter can read his lines straight across the camera lens. Thus he can speak earnestly and directly into the eyes of the viewer at home, while the operator, often a girl, keeps pace by 'rolling' the lines as he speaks them.

In the old days the giant roll of yellow lavatory paper with large type on it was fixed either just above or just below the lens and all of us were taught 'tricks' to conceal the fact that we were reading rather than speaking. The best known trick is the glance upwards or the glance sideways – or even the gesture of taking off one's spectacles.

I once passed that advice on to a brand new reporter on 'This Week'. He was frightened he wouldn't remember, so hypnotized did he feel he would become by the words rolling in front of him. He decided to put a note to himself on autocue – lots of performers do.

On that Thursday night in 1963 I saw with pleasure the lesson put into practice. The young man, a slightly self-important graduate destined for the House of Commons, where he now serves among many like himself, was in the middle of a far too long speech about the state of one of the social services.

In his eagerness, he read on and on; pompously, remorselessly. About half-way through the piece he drew breath and studiously said: 'Take off glasses, look concerned.'

There was a long, long pause. His eyes rolled desperately, and then he plunged on with his piece. He was a much nicer man to know after that.

My 'comeuppance' was delivered by a beautiful blonde autocue operator called Sabina. She had decided that I was taking her work too much for granted. I was, and she took her revenge. We were broadcasting 'live' a two-and-a-half-hour long 'Man Alive' debate on the future of education. The studio was crowded with the most distinguished parliamentarians and educationalists. Everybody, it seemed, was a Sir or a Lady, if not a Lord.

It was hard work, particularly for a reporter whose formal education had stopped at the age of fourteen. Half-way through the discussion the time came for me to introduce the next piece of film. At this stage, the reporter invariably swivels in his chair and gazes at his camera, expecting the loyal autocue operator to have his next line ready in the mirrored device in front of the lens. I calmed the debate, swivelled and turned to camera.

In the autocue frame were the handwritten words: 'Blow us a kiss or I won't roll a thing.'

I'm told a squint of terror appeared on my face and my Adam's apple was seen to bob ineffectively up and down. I opened my mouth. The words in the frame didn't move. Nothing came out of my mouth. What were my next lines? What was I due to say? I couldn't recall one word.

I pursed my lips and, with an expression of dying agony, made a 'moue' at the camera. My first line appeared.

I tried to read it as though I'd just controlled a coughing fit. I don't think I fooled anybody. It certainly didn't fool Sabina – and I never neglected her again.

5 On the road

David Frost wasn't a bad researcher when he got his first job in television, except for his habit of turning up alarmingly late for work in the morning and his belief that the reason would make you love him more. He had, invariably, been up until four in the morning performing in cabaret at the Establishment or the Blue Angel, both centre pieces of the spirit of the early sixties.

Frost, fresh and cheekily down from Cambridge, as well as a young lady fresh and not so cheekily up from Reading were the first two (and I think the last two) management trainees hired directly from college by Associated Rediffusion, who were anxious to introduce graduate enthusiasm among the ranks of cynical journalistic experience. The girl, Sue Turner, went on to become Head of Children's Programmes and a great success. David Frost grew and grew. In those days it was my job to teach young David Frost about life 'on the road', film locations.

As a researcher he had to discover and organize the people and places for filming 'This Week' items. I spent the morning instructing him in the delicate balances that exist once a film crew is on the road. I made sure that he also understood his priority was to see that the reporter was comforted and cared for more than anybody. And off he went on his first story, to Leicester, where they were about to open the largest supermarket in England.

As the reporter, I was due to join him twenty-four hours later with the film crew, by which time he should have researched the facts, found likely interviewees and arranged accommodation for all of us. I knew the last bit would be difficult because every grocery executive in the country had descended on Leicester for the grand preview of the grandest market ever. But Frost didn't fail.

We arrived in Leicester, drove to the best hotel where we were expected. Not only were we expected but the manager himself showed me to my room. It wasn't just a room, it was the Bridal Suite. A giant canopied double bed draped with apricot coloured silk, an appalling sea-green sitting room, a bathroom containing the largest mauve bidet I've ever seen, at least six huge bunches of flowers and a gigantic basket of fruit.

The manager was positively obsequious. I was deeply suspicious, being more used to curt dismissals and complaints about my film teams.

'Are you full?' I asked.

'Oh yes, sir, not a spare room in the place. But nothing's too good for you. We understand perfectly. About everything. Don't you worry.'

And on that mysterious note he walked from the room. Only after he'd left did I realize he had left the room in a crablike movement, almost walking backwards. I must be going mad I thought.

In the dining room at dinner time (we were to film the next day) the manager reappeared at my elbow. So did champagne, 'on the house'. Even the film crew, cynical and weary in the ways of the world, were impressed. I attempted to remain boot-faced but, in the end, could stand it no longer.

'David,' I said, 'why have I got the bridal suite and all this amazing personal service? What is going on?'

'It's because you're famous, old boy. They really love "This Week" up here. They're fans to a man. The hotel practically grinds to a halt whenever you're on the screen. I've had to be most stern with them about not pestering you for autographs. You know it's the price of success. You must learn to live with it, Desmond.'

I almost believed him, except for the tiniest unresolved niggling at the back of my mind. But as the evening wore on, even that minute doubt vanished.

On my way out to the lift to go to my room for the night, the manager bounced out from behind the service door.

'Now, don't you worry about a thing, sir. It's all going to be all right. I've warned the right people and I've left the back door to the kitchen unlocked and ajar.'

With that, he vanished. David was with me. In the lift I rounded on him. 'What the hell is going on? Is this one of your jokes? Be serious. We're here to work, you know.'

He looked thoughtful and didn't answer for a long time. Then he said: 'I *am* taking the job seriously and I *am* doing my best for you. But there wasn't a room to be had anywhere in the town and I didn't want to fail you.'

An awful feeling began to creep over me.

'What did you do?'

'Well, it's worked hasn't it?' he said defensively. 'I only told a small romanticism. And after all it's one that will really liven them up. Shouldn't be surprised if they don't remember it all their lives, even tell their grandchildren about it.'

'What romanticism?'

'I just happened to notice that it's not too far from Sandringham. So I swore the manager to secrecy and said you were having a passionate affair with a royal lady who would be visiting you in the middle of the night and could he see that the crew were in another part of the hotel and that you were in suitable accommodation ...'

With that we reached the door of the bridal suite and he left me.

In fact my own initiation into location filming still brings pinkness to my face at the memory of my gauche ignorance.

We had been despatched, in 1960, to Eastbourne to make a film about a Civil Defence training site. I had been only two weeks in television and this was my first film and here we all were in the Grand Hotel. The director wore a trilby on the back of his head throughout dinner and had previously distinguished himself as the best director they'd ever had on a studio 'pop' programme called 'Cool for Cats'. He hadn't made many films but he was very, very cool. There was a film crew that seemed to number twenty but was, in fact, ten, a harrassed and conscientious researcher and a blonde production assistant.

She proved to be a fascinating dinner companion and I became intensely absorbed by the story of her boyfriend who treated her so badly.

At 1.00 a.m. that morning there was a knock on my door. When I opened it the lovely blonde lady was there.

'I know it's late, but I have this dreadful headache and I wondered if you'd got any aspirin with you,' she said.

There I was, fresh from Fleet Street, (a male and beery place) and, what's more, I didn't have any aspirin. She was such a lovely girl and I did want to help.

'I'm afraid I don't have any, but the director is just across the corridor in Room 203. You could try him,' I suggested.

It was a long time before I learned to understand the look that crossed her face in the hotel corridor in the small hours of that morning.

I also have to report that it is almost impossible to remain innocent on film locations. I failed to achieve the impossible. Indeed, by the time I was sent, by 'This Week', with a film crew, to Stockholm for the New Year's Eve celebrations I had lost a great deal of that early naivety, willingly and gloriously.

We were going to Stockholm because Great Britain was on the brink of introducing stern drink-driving penalties and the breathalyser. In Scandinavia both the penalties and the breathalyser had existed for some time but that didn't stop all the hard-drinking Swedes from having a marvellous New Year's Eve. They would just select a member of each party to remain sober, or hire someone else to be their non-drinking driver.

We booked into a small but modern hotel and drove to Stockholm's grandest hotel, where we set up to film the New Year's Eve ball and arranged to interview some of the guests. Margaret, the production assistant, turned up for work later that evening in a full-length crocheted black dress. Concentrating on work was going to be difficult. The rest of us stood around in our Moss Bros dinner jackets waiting for the party to warm up.

The director rushed everywhere making the shape of a picture frame with his hands and uttering extravagant cooing noises in order to draw attention to himself and the fact that he *was* the director; a gesture I considered over the top in the country that produced Ingmar Bergman.

We filmed the interviews; and couples dancing; and many people drinking; and some individuals miserably and studiously not drinking. We filmed the band playing; and the decorations glittering; and cars waiting in the frost; and snow outside; and any other thing that the director thought might contribute to his opportunity to shoot a full-length feature film for a ten-minute slot in a weekly magazine programme. Finally, even he ran out of ideas and his fingers, still held in the shape of a picture frame, were beginning to get cramp.

We were to spend the next morning filming in the police headquarters laboratory, where blood samples were analysed, and I was to get scientifically drunk, one whisky at a time, while measurements were taken. Not at that time of day and in that particular way, a prospect to look forward to. But, in the meantime, we were free to enjoy ourselves and the ball.

I danced with the production assistant. She really was very good looking but I hadn't too much hope. By now I had become a realist about the silly games played on film locations. While I like to think myself attractive, personable, a kind of journalistic Van Johnson, I knew I wasn't the debonair, bowl-a-lady-off-her-feet, Cary Grant figure that it would obviously take to win the affections of the lovely Margaret. But:

'How would you normally spend New Year's Eve?' she asked.

'I can't think of anything nicer than a bottle of iced champagne, and two glasses,' I said, still being Van Johnson.

'That's what I'd most like, too. Do you think you could organize it in your room?'

I could hardly believe it. I led her back to the table and sped off to make a phone call to my hotel. I managed to get through to an English-speaking hall porter. I explained what I needed, virtually promised him a pension for life if he would have the champagne and the glasses, and a bowl of fruit, taken up to my room immediately. He said yes.

Back at the ball, I took Margaret on to the dance floor once more.

'All fixed, exactly as you suggested. Any time you want to leave.' I was becoming more like Cary Grant by the minute. Even my dancing seemed smoother, or perhaps she'd just learned to keep her feet out of the way.

Ten minutes later we took a cab across a starlit, snowy Stockholm. We sat without speaking in the back, the message – and the future – clear and understood between us. By God, this was better than drinking beer in Fleet Street any day. At the hotel Margaret asked 'What's your room number?' I told her.

'I'll be there in ten minutes.'

In my room I tore off my clothes. I rubbed aftershave all over me. And then, for two full minutes, I hopped around the room in agony. I had never before experienced the effect of raw spirit on the more sensitive parts of the body.

I had been given, for Christmas, a grey silk Austin Reed dressing gown, very 'Cary Grant'. I tied, and retied, the sash at least a dozen times, adjusted the lighting and set the champagne bottle at the right angle in the ice bucket, I wasn't very good at this, but I was trying, by God I was trying.

A few minutes later there was a tap on the door. Tugging

once more at the sash of my dressing gown, I opened the door. Margaret stood framed in the light from the corridor, in a white negligee.

She moved into the room, and turned her head to glance over her shoulder. 'All right boys, the party's in here,' she said suddenly in a loud voice. And the rest of the crew, thoughtfully clutching their own glasses, walked into the room behind her roaring and whooping at the sight of my dressing gown and my bare legs beneath it.

In front of me the dancing eyes of Margaret gazed coolly at my total small boy discomfiture. I was no longer Cary Grant, probably not even Van Johnson. Harpo Marx perhaps?

They finished the champagne. They told me, over and over again, how they had planned with glee the New Year's Eve 'seduction'. And they were kind enough to call me a 'good sport'. Margaret was, by this time, twined, like a boa constrictor, round the handsome assistant cameraman. And they all left. There was one orange still in the fruit bowl. I peeled it – reflecting that it should have been a lemon.

In spite of it all, film locations are the most enjoyable part of television. They can also be horrendous, exhausting, fraught with rows and tensions, leaving you on return to base swearing never to travel with a film crew again; only to be found cheerfully packing passport and clean shirts a few days later.

Shortly after Esther had started appearing on 'Braden's Week' she did a six months' stint as a reporter on 'Nationwide'. The pace on a nightly magazine programme is excruciating. There is no time for finesse, no room for mistakes in the pressure of filling the day's quota of stories.

And of all the films stories most beloved by producers on daily magazine programmes, those about animals and strange and curious pets are top of the league.

If you own a goldfish that whistles, a budgerigar that roller skates, a duck that goes shopping with you, a dog that answers the telephone, a cow that dances to 'Rule Britannia', a tabby cat that plays ping pong, then telephone programmes like 'Nationwide' or 'That's Life!'. A film crew will arrive, urgent and panting on your doorstep, almost before you've replaced the receiver. The British, it seems, have developed a tradition of idiosyncratic and eccentric pets – and a ratings-conscious desire to see them on television.

This time it was a talented duck, owned by a farmer's wife, the pride of her children and a source of amazement to her neighbours in the village. The duck not only followed the farmer's wife everywhere, even to the shops, but insisted on barking like a dog every time it saw either a dog or a cat.

The story had almost limitless opportunities for film shots. The crew leapt into a station wagon like a fire brigade answering an emergency call.

'If we film quickly this morning and get back before lunch we can process it and transmit it today,' said the director. 'Day-for-day' filming is the most hectic kind of 'Nationwide' location. But the challenge of bringing the talented duck to the viewers, before rival programmes, or Fleet Street tabloids could hear of its star quality, was strong. They sped off.

Thirty miles from London they tore into the drive of the farmhouse and halted in front of the door, gravel spinning from the wheels.

The door opened and a lady, obviously the farmer's wife, appeared in a state of high excitement and anticipation.

'We're from "Nationwide",' explained the director unnecessarily. 'We came at once. Now there's no need to get overexcited. It's all in a day's work for us and you'll find it easy to make a film.'

The crew were busy unloading camera and tripod. The farmer's wife started to push past the crew to walk down the drive away from them.

It dawned on the director that her reaction was something more than just the stunned anticipation of a woman about to take part in a television film. The farmer's wife was obviously in a state of shock rather than excitement.

'What's wrong? Have you had bad news?' asked the director.

'It's Dabber. Dabber the duck. I must go and see,' she said.

'He isn't being filmed by someone else? Thames Television haven't got here already, have they?' he asked, fearing the worst.

'No, it's not that. He was down by the gate to the road, barking at a cat,' said the farmer's wife.

'Oh Lord, he hasn't lost his voice has he?'

'No, no. But you've just run over him.' She ran towards the road.

She was too late. Nothing could save Dabber. His eccentric tricks would now never make him nationally known. The farmer's wife had lost more than her talented duck, she had lost her place in the television 'record book' of loony pets and loving owners. Now, nobody would stop her in the street, there would be no fan mail from strangers, no fame.

Silently, the crew put the tripod, camera and equipment back in the station wagon. Helplessly, the director gestured his sympathy and inadequacy. They climbed in, turned the station wagon round and drove off slowly.

Looking back through the rear window the director could see the farmer's wife still standing there, bereft, her duck dead, her opportunity lost.

Esther believes that cats are the most difficult of all animals to film on location. I'm sure she's right as they are clearly the most intelligent and admirable creatures, easily capable of assessing – and rejecting – the idiot behaviour of humans in film crews. Nevertheless, where would a programme like 'That's Life!' be without the regular appearance of performing cats?

It was Esther who told me that on one particular day, remembered in film production history, a film crew, shooting a cat food commercial, used up all the existing stock of a particular kind of film available in the whole country – and still didn't get the moggy of their choice to eat the meal they put in front of him.

Despite this awesome warning, she and her co-producer, Henry Murray, decided to run a consumer test on cat food.

They invited every member of the team who had a cat, or could borrow a cat, to turn up at the house of Esther's friend Deirdre, who owned the most independent cat in the United Kingdom, Mrs MacLean. Henry Murray arrived with the film crew, a dozen pet food bowls and a vast supply of different pet foods.

The consumer survey was not meant to be precise, statistical or scientific, but rather a rewarding and (only perhaps) revealing occasion.

Everybody had forgotten that Mrs MacLean was a vicious, claws out, untamed monster who had already savaged some of the most famous names in the country and was obviously looking forward to demolishing all the other cats and their owners. What's more, Mrs MacLean would only eat anything at all if her owner shrieked 'Beefies' over and over again in a high falsetto. It was Mrs MacLean's home so she could not be excluded.

In the course of filming that consumer survey, Henry was clawed several times, badly enough to need attention from the BBC's first aid room; the film camera ran, for minutes on end, on the sight of Deirdre and Esther and Henry peering under furniture and calling for Mrs MacLean to come out; four other cats had been taken home by their aggrieved owners; and the pet food was going dry and curly in the neglected bowls. The final film was, however, memorable. Not so much a consumer survey – more a savage comedy.

Mind you, if Esther had been forgetful on one foreign film location, we wouldn't be writing this book together – and she'd be the sixth wife of a polygamous Mormon in Utah.

She was working as the reporter on a documentary about Mormons in Salt Lake City when, after much secret to-ing and fro-ing and one occasion when they had been fired at with a shotgun, she and the director Peter Chafer were promised an interview with a man who had several wives. At that time it was not only illegal, in America, to have several wives but it was also unpopular. Hence the shotgun and the secrecy.

They drove out into the country with their guide to a large

pleasant ranch-type home. The man of the house met them. He was impressive. Of course, anybody with five wives would be but 'John' was also six feet six inches tall, bearded and worked as a private detective, a job that somehow didn't take him away from home on too many nights.

In the sitting room the atmosphere seemed, even to strangers from British television, more than a little strained. Six ladies sat round in uncomfortable silence. One of them, older than the rest, suddenly spoke.

'I'm Sylvia's mother and I don't approve of it,' she announced firmly. It turned out that she was the mother of John's latest bride and somehow her daughter and her new son-in-law had 'forgotten' until that moment to mention the fact that 'John' was a Mormon and his newest bride was wife number five.

Wife number one, a pleasant looking woman in her thirties, took Esther on a guided tour of this Mormon household. Each wife had a neat pine-walled bedroom and a comfortable double bed, with a charming wedding picture on the bedside table; a different wedding picture by each bed, of course. The basement had been turned into a keep fit gymnasium for John. Obviously a necessary arrangement.

Esther chatted with the senior wife and discovered that between them all there were nine children. The revealing thing was that all the wives seemed to enjoy the arrangement. They had worked out, between them, a rota for all domestic duties and chores. When some of them were pregnant it meant that 'John' spent more time in the keep fit den, or with the other wives, because under Mormon practice, apparently, you don't 'bother' your wife if she is expecting a child.

The number one wife showed much curiosity about Esther, questioned her about her work and life at home in England. Finally, she said: 'Sister Esther, have you ever considered why the good Lord has preserved you in this unmarried state until now?' Sister Esther had considered the matter but had certainly not decided that the good Lord intended her spinster days to finish in Utah. As they say in all the best Sunday papers – she made her excuses and left.

A 'ghoster' is nothing to be frightened of and a 'flyer' has no connection with aeroplanes. But, like 'bubble' and 'rate', as well as 'allowance', and 'three-fifths', and 'penalty', they all add up to money for the crews 'on the road'.

Long ago the trade unions, who protect film technicians from the sort of exploitations that happened in the twenties and thirties, moved into a position of strength and attack, rather than weakness and defence. The jargon, agreed between them and television management, is the way both sides describe payments made for nights spent away from home, for lunch breaks that start too late, for allowances abroad and many other golden compensations.

'Flyers' are the method by which crews claim an overnight allowance but actually manage to drive to their homes, and back again in the morning, while charging as though they'd spent the night in a hotel. 'Ghosters' are the payments made when a crew has worked so late in the evening, and is called so early the next day, that it is not possible to give them a minimum of ten hours between stopping and starting again. The penalty for this is to pay for an extra day's work that never actually takes place, called a 'ghoster'.

The 'rate' and the 'allowance' are both the scales of payments for overnight accommodation and food. In foreign countries the allowance is designed to cover hotel and meals. But if – as often happens – a clever producer has arranged for the crew to stay at a hotel free of charge with meals included, the crew will still be entitled to charge 'three-fifths', that is three-fifths of the allowance – even though they're not paying a penny for accommodation or food. They receive this on the grounds, negotiated by their union representatives, that their 'free choice' has been taken away from them. They may not like the hotel bedrooms or agree with the meals on the table d'hote section of the menu. A 'penalty' is the fixed payment, or 'fine', paid by management if a director is even as much as one minute late in breaking the crew for lunch.

I'd only been with the BBC a week or two and was visiting a film location in Essex, when the unit electrician came up to me. 'What's your grade mate?' he said. I didn't know. I knew I was a programme editor and I asked him if he knew what that meant in this strange, new terminology. He clearly did and the answer, equally clearly, pleased him.

'Okay, you lot,' he said to the crew round him. 'The overnight allowance goes up, we've got management level on the road with us.'

Just by visiting that location I had cost the BBC, and my programme budget, money, because everybody could claim living expenses at a higher level. It was a long time before I realized that for the same reason researchers and secretaries liked to know which train I was travelling on. If I was entitled to First Class travel then they could claim it too when they were with me. On their own the class conscious BBC designates them as Second Class travellers. In fact, they would usually buy a cheap day return, sit in the first class restaurant car with me and charge a full first class return. I always thought them so poorly paid, I never minded their small profit-making.

Most film crews, too, don't want the increased comfort of better hotels or better class travel. Oh no, they want the difference − in cash. If you want to discover where the cheapest boarding houses are, and what the most economical travelling methods are, ask a film crew. Very few cameramen and sound men would prefer to stay in a posh hotel. They'd rather take home the difference between a high allowance and the cost of cheap digs.

Once in Hollywood James Kenelm Clarke, the director, and I wanted to stay with the crew. We were shooting a difficult and demanding documentary in the 'Americans' series about a private eye. The cameraman was a great personal friend, as was the sound recordist; and we felt it would improve the quality of our work if, when the day's shooting was over, we could all still be together socially.

What that meant, in the end, was the director and I had to stay at the same place as the crew, not the other way round (although the BBC overseas allowance for Los Angeles was generous enough to have afforded us all a very good hotel, if we had wanted it).

We wound up in Sunset Boulevard itself, but not the Beverly Hills end. We were booked into the Oasis Motor Inn. Very exotic it sounded, too, on my travel form. But the reality was something else. I think I was probably the first person to have spent more than forty-five minutes in my room.

The motel appeared to be almost totally occupied by a permanent community of tired young ladies in 'hot pants', who drove small sports cars, came and went very frequently and kept bodyguards, with ferocious moustaches and very sharp clothes, outside their rooms.

At the reception desk, as I signed in, a man with an auburn wig, which had slipped slightly, asked me if I wanted to borrow any 'ditty books' to take to my room. Why, I thought, would I want song sheets? Or was it a naval expression like 'ditty bag'? Anyway, I nodded and he gave me a bundle of books.

In my room I gazed bleakly at the visible cost of my desire for community life with the film crew. There were stains on the walls, burns on the furniture, the bedroom telephone, stretched out to the full length of its cord, sat on a soiled patch of carpet still four feet from the bed, three wire hangers were twisted round each other on a single metal rail outside the broken cubicle shower. No wonder the room was only $12 a night (an average hotel room in Los Angeles at that time would have been $23 and the BBC allowance was $50 a night).

I threw my suitcase and the 'ditty books' on the bed. I saw then that they weren't 'ditty' books – they were *dirty* books, very dirty books. A thoughtful management was including 'hard core' extras for its customers who, it was clear, did not normally consist of film crews and reporters working for the BBC.

We stuck it out. Apart from the sound of fights, and the disputes about payment in the middle of the night, and regular siren-wailing visits from the vice patrol, it was an interesting experience. Once it was appreciated by the other semi-permanent residents, and their watchful guardians, that we weren't a new kinky group from England poaching on their business preserves we became regarded as affectionate mascots for the place.

Messages about footages, exposures and the flight details of our film 'rushes' were faithfully copied down and relayed to us by the ladies in 'hot pants'. The crew enjoyed the swimming pool, when off duty, on what was virtually an exclusive basis – the ladies were too busy to be able to use it. And we won the unstinted admiration of private eye John O'Grady, whose life story we were filming, when we told him where we were staying.

'You guys have got to be either tough or broke – or both,' he told us. But there was a possibility he had left out. We were living on the 'rate' – and making a profit. We were a crew 'on the road'.

Viewers picture life on the road as glamorous, exotic, weeks by the pool in Jamaica. Not in our experience. It can be more than unglamorous but at least you see life. Once, at a hotel in England, Esther checked in with a film crew for a sequence on one of 'The Big Time' programmes. Minutes later she was back at the reception desk. 'I'm afraid my room hasn't been made up,' she said.

'Impossible madam. Nobody's used that room for weeks.'

She invited the manager to accompany her upstairs. Together they gazed at the unmade bed and the ashtray full of cigarette stubs in the centre of the sheet. There was a bottle and three glasses on the bedside table. 'Excuse me a minute, I'm sorry about this,' said the manager.

As Esther descended to the bar to wait for the allocation of a new room, or the cleaning of the existing one, she overheard the sound of a row going on, in the spirit and tones of a scene from 'Fawlty Towers'. The manager was bellowing at two young waiters: 'I've told you before. Your private life is your own affair, I suppose. But in future if I find you've been using guest rooms I'll throw buckets of water over each of you.'

At dinner in the hotel that night she couldn't help noticing two very subdued waiters moving around the dining room. Then the head waiter appeared at her elbow. She did a double take. He was wearing a purple shirt, strong perfume, a gold bracelet, an earring and what appeared to be rouge.

He, too, seemed very subdued.

I'm forever grateful when I remember that all that I know about good food and good wine I've been taught by members of film crews, while on location. One cameraman introduced me to two wines, now among my favourites, Gerwurtztramminer and Sancerre. A sound recordist, just about the most travelled man I've ever met, taught me how to enjoy Japanese food. A lighting electrician showed me how to discover the best local shopping plazas in American towns, in order to search for take-home bargains in bed linen and kitchen equipment.

Film crews always seem to travel with copies of the airline guide and they know the regulations better than most booking clerks.

If you are returning home from an arduous film trip abroad, they will show you how to use your entitled 'fifteen per cent deviation' from the scheduled flight path to spend a day or two in exotic little backwaters like Bermuda.

Film crews always know the international telephone dialing codes from any country back to London. If you're ever kept waiting, in somebody's office abroad, or anywhere where there is a telephone, you will rapidly hear the sound of loyal film technicians speaking to their wives and children affectionately and domestically on somebody else's phone.

Do I make us all sound like swarms of locusts or bands of pirates? Then I don't mean to. Film crews may be, for some tastes, outrageous but in my experience they are also affectionate, loyal, hard-working, usually intensely absorbed in the story they are filming and the best kind of people in the world with whom to be away from home. They produce the finest camera work and the clearest sound, they are responsible for documentary stories that move and delight you, artistic craftsmanship frequently shot under arduous conditions. So if there are 'ghosters' and 'flyers' they are earned and deserved.

If you go on the road with a film crew you may learn about life in the raw – but if you take an outside broadcast unit, with all its electronic paraphernalia, you may learn lessons you didn't expect. Cilla Black, a lovely, bouncy, singing success from Liverpool, decided during one of her BBC television series, that it would be fun for the viewers if she were to bring a little of the flavour of life 'on the road' to their screens. Her production team arranged for an outside broadcast unit to go, secretly, during each live show to a mystery location, which would only be revealed when watching viewers suddenly realized it was their home or their life being shown on the screen.

They 'piloted' one such occasion, as an experiment, in her first programme. It was a roaring success. They stuck a camera on Shepherd's Bush Green, just outside the Television Theatre from which the programme was broadcast, and invited viewers to bring along their pet dogs to meet each other and then be questioned about them by Cilla, while she was still in the Television Theatre and they were in the night air.

It was the biggest dog fight in the world. It was accompanied by Cilla, entreating the uncaring dogs, savaging each other to: 'Be friends, please be friends.'

But it was a wondrous sight – and it was certainly responsible for the dramatic increase in the programme's ratings the following week.

Next Saturday, the cameras were waiting in the darkness in a back street of a Northern town. An outside broadcast crew with electronic cameras and studio style control equipment is a different kettle of fish from a film crew. It consists of several huge vans and as many as forty men. It's not easy to hide an OB in the dark. But they managed. At the appropriate moment in the programme Cilla beamed at the cameras and told the television audience: 'Outside in the dark somewhere there are cameras and a crew. They could be outside your home. We're going to switch on the lights now and if you recognize your house, come to the front door and wave to us. Invite our crew in and I'll talk to you.'

The lights switched on to reveal a typical 'Coronation Street' terraced house. The windows were curtained and dead-looking, the door firmly shut. In the studio Cilla called out to the family that she courageously assumed to be watching the BBC, and her, behind the curtains:

'Come on out, show yourselves.'

No response.

She ad libbed quite well for a minute or two about people hiding from the cameras – 'Or maybe they're too busy,' she added with a giggle. Then they sent in the stage manager, wearing his headphones and carrying a microphone. Even though he must have known he was 'in vision' as he approached the front door, he still adopted that posture natural to all studio and outside broadcast technicians who have been trained never to be caught in front of the camera; it's a kind of hunched half-run, head down, shoulders up, as though he's being shot at.

He knocked at the door – and waited. He knocked again – and turned to the camera, still hunched, and gave a thumbs down signal to show there was no reply. At that moment the door opened a couple of inches and a face appeared in the crack. Cilla's voice boomed into the floodlit street: 'Come on luv, open up, it's Cilla Black here. Won't you ask us in for a word or two?'

The door opened fully, the stage manager, still with headphones and microphone was admitted, followed by a hand-held camera and the other technicians.

In the tiny, crowded sitting room, promptly flooded with white light from a portable TV lamp, a number of men and women could indistinctly be seen, sitting on sofas and chairs in a state of wriggling embarrassment. They were quite evidently overwhelmed by the visit of 'the telly' to their home.

There also seemed to be a lot of them for such a small home.

Still booming from the loudspeakers Cilla, back in the studio in Shepherd's Bush, started to interview them.

In reply to her not very demanding questions like 'Who are you?' 'What do you do?' and 'Didn't you realize we'd put your house on telly?' she got embarrassed non-committal answers, almost monosyllabic.

But Cilla is a game girl, she pressed on. The fourth person she spoke to was gazing anywhere but at the camera. 'That's a nice suntan you've got, have you just come back from holiday?' she shouted. The question produced, finally, animation on the faces of the people in the picture, even amusement.

'No, most of us have nice suntans back home in Jamaica,' he said. The audience loved it.

Some time after the broadcast Cilla and the production team learned that the house they had surprised was actually a brothel, the people they had attempted to interview were customers and working ladies who had quite certainly *not* been watching BBC Television at the moment the arc lights were switched on outside.

But bravely, Cilla and her team pressed on with what they felt was a good idea. The next week 'live on the air', the cameras were poised in darkness, the technicians waiting to leap into action, in a car park alongside a tower block of flats in the Midlands.

On cue the floodlights came on, Cilla's voice boomed through the winter night and the camera zoomed slowly and remorselessly in to a sixth floor balcony. The curtain remained drawn, the door closed. Suddenly, the door was flung open and a man and a woman erupted on to the balcony gazing with terrified disbelief at what they obviously thought to be a Russian invasion or the beginning of an IRA hostage siege.

Cilla's voice asked, 'Wave to us if you were watching my programme on television.' There was no wave, but there was a frenzied consultation between the man and the woman.

They turned in fatalistic surrender towards the light, gesturing but unheard. Cilla chatted on and then she hesitated.

It had suddenly dawned on her, as well as millions of delighted viewers, that the man was in what appeared to be shirttails and the woman was wrapped in a sheet. They really had been disturbed. It was time for Cilla to say goodnight. She did, cheerfully, making a joke of the moment.

Again, it was some time before Cilla, and the production team, discovered the truth. The lady's husband, it turned out, was away on business. And the gentleman had not expected floodlights and cameras to interrupt his evening with her.

So, the score so far added up to: the biggest dog fight in the country; a visit to a disorderly house; an affair discovered. The viewing figures for the programme were increasing by leaps and bounds. But so, too, were the numbers of complaints from people caught in Cilla's 'surprise'. The item was dropped.

I've always thought it a pity, it seemed to me that a whole new series could have developed from it. Indeed, it might even have replaced the licence system. Transmitted nightly with the title 'If you're up to no good, pay the money – otherwise give us a wave', it could have set new standards for television; the guardian of morality, by threat.

One greatly embarrassing moment 'on the road' for me never reached an audience. Fortunately, when you're working with film crews or videorecording, you can reduce by editing the number of 'egg-on-face' situations you have to live with on the air.

I was filming with the American 82nd Airborne Division, a body of proud, highly trained warriors, known as 'America's Guard of Honor'. For one of the 'Americans' series we were making a profile of the tough and likeable veteran who led these men, Major-General Thomas H. Tackaberry, one of the most distinguished American generals. When I needed a bite from which to speak the camera statement introducing the Division, it was his idea to choose the toughest part of the commando assault course in their training camp, Fort Bragg, North Carolina.

The instructors on that assault course, men apparently made from tungsten and titanium, pointed with glee to the most difficult handicap in the whole course. It was a huge tree trunk mounted on a kind of parallel bars over which the paratroopers had to launch themselves head first – with one sadistic extra element. Two other paratroopers would roll the tree trunk towards the running soldier in order to try and catch him in the most painful part of his midriff, at precisely the moment he was jumping forward to dive over the obstacle. With careful timing a soldier could just avoid permanent emasculation, land on a forward roll and then run to the next obstacle. An impressive display of strength, courage and skill.

A squad of thirty of America's finest, their heads virtually shaved, their backs ramrod stiff, waited – panting from the exertions of the earlier part of the assault course – for me to start speaking to camera before they were cued forward by their instructors to provide a dramatic background to the introductory statement.

I started speaking. The men were cued, so were the two men rolling the tree trunk.

'These men are the bravest of the brave, the toughest of the tough,' I intoned to camera. There was a thud and a strangled noise behind me.

I continued. 'In order to achieve a peak of fitness and athletic skill not matched anywhere else in the American army,' another thud, a scraping noise and something that sounded like a groan.

'They train night and day to be in a state of instant readiness to take on anything that may threaten their country.' Pounding feet and there was no doubt about it this time. The running feet, the scraping and rolling of the log had been followed by a scream. Quickly stifled but, nevertheless, a scream.

I pressed on and finished the camera statement. The director called cut. I turned to look at the cause of the thuds and groans that had been going on behind me.

The ground was covered with men crawling painfully

away. Even as I watched, the next recruit ran towards the log which caught him full in the chest and hurled him back to the ground. Not one soldier had cleared the obstacle.

I admire James Kenelm Clarke, the director, greatly. He managed to keep a straight face while standing directly in my eyeline, able to see the extent of the disaster going on behind my back. Later, we shot the camera statement again with the men swarming up a thirty-foot high scrambling net and tumbling down the other side. On the screen, it was very impressive but the other version found its way, inevitably, into the film editor's Christmas party film. That's the occasion on which 364 days of hard work in the cutting room are made worthwhile by the showing of all those awful boobs that take place 'on the road'.

Production assistants – the television equivalent of continuity girls – are essential 'on the road'. They are a calming, steadying influence, whose organizational skills ensure that the production team and the film crew work and travel comfortably. They have a whole range of production responsibilities and they deserve the odd bonus, like a good dinner in a nice hotel.

Once, travelling to Budleigh Salterton for a film interview, we had to call at the home of our production assistant, Carol, to collect her. She'd overslept. The director was cross and she was flustered. But it only delayed us by five minutes and we were on our way.

That night, in the bar of the Grand Hotel, we met for a drink with the crew before dinner in the Palm Court Restaurant where a resident trio could be heard sawing a painful way through their repertoire. Carol was at the bar and seemed even more flustered than she had been that morning. And our director was clearly now cross about something else.

She told me: 'In the rush I forgot to pack a decent dress. I've only come out with a spare pair of jeans and another sweater. Tom's cross with me because the restaurant is rather posh and he thinks we'll be refused admission because I'm not in a dress.'

'Leave it to me. It's not your fault, could have happened to anyone. Worry not.'

I clapped our director on the shoulder and said: 'Come on, let's help the girl. It's time for Sir Galahads.'

I suggested that we all gather around Carol, rather like secret service men round the President of the United States, and move in the direction of the Palm Court Restaurant. A stern looking head waiter stood in the doorway, in white tie and tails.

Only Carol's head could be seen between us as we crabbed along like a fourteen-legged mutant with forced and noisy jollity. But still the head waiter's hand came up like a traffic policeman.

'Excuse me, sir,' he said in tones of doom. 'I'm afraid you can't enter the restaurant.'

There was nothing for it except to try a bluff. In my coldest manner, not just icy, but glacial, I said: 'I would prefer not to be too close to the music and I would be grateful if you personally would show us to the table, which we have reserved.'

That, I thought, would forestall any noises about whether Carol was wearing a dress. But the head waiter was not to be deflected.

'You can't go in, sir. We really can't have gentlemen in our dining room wearing sports jackets,' he said looking at my houndstooth special. Half an hour later I joined my colleagues at dinner, wearing a suit, sulking mightily, to find that I had been given the chair nearest the bass fiddle at our table, which was next to the band. Game, set and match to the head waiter – and still nobody had noticed or commented on Carol's jeans.

Life on the road sometimes has real risks attached. Esther was on the road – or, more precisely, out on the streets – when she was arrested.

She is usually extremely law abiding and had no suspicion when she went to conduct a consumer test into bat stew in the street market at North End Road, West London, that she would be committing a crime.

She and her team choose regularly to film in that particular street market because there are a great many delightful characters there who can provide them with instant jokes – and also send them up rotten. The film team usually stand on a corner where they can see the people coming and going, and can, in turn, be seen themselves. The ones who stop are the ones who want to play the game. Esther admits they aren't very popular with the stall holders. They are an odd breed – dressed in scuffed plimsolls and ragged T-shirts. We are told they often go home to palatial mansions in the suburbs where they polish their shiny new Rolls Royces. Whether that is true or not, they certainly take money extremely seriously and resent deeply the fact that Esther may be distracting their customers.

But this particular morning she was greeted with smiles as they decanted the bat stew into little glass bowls and got handfuls of plastic teaspoons together. Esther was talking to a lovely Welsh lady who was screwing up her face with horrified anticipation when she saw two policemen walking towards her. One was very young and had a brand new moustache trying to get out. The other was rather elderly and florid. At first it seemed as though they were going to walk by, and Esther was surprised when the older policeman turned and came back waving his arm.

'Move back there,' he said.

'Pardon,' she said.

'You can't do that there, you're blocking the whole pavement.'

'But I've been doing this here for twelve years.'

'Well, you're not doing it today, move back there or I'll arrest you,' he said.

Esther and team, still completely baffled because the police have always been very benevolent towards their street carnivals, took four steps back down the side road and the little Welsh lady followed them. They continued to discuss the qualities of bat stew. Ten minutes later the policeman was back.

'I told you to move,' he said.

'I did move,' Esther said.

'Well, I've warned you, you're blocking the pavement,' he said. And he left.

Esther and the crew decided to move across the road to a different corner which was a bit wider. After a while eight or ten people gathered around the steaming pots of stew guessing what was in it. Frog said one man, mouse said another. Suddenly the two policemen were there.

'You're under arrest,' said the older policeman.

Esther says she couldn't believe her ears. The camera was still running and through the eye piece the cameraman could easily see that the pavement was quite unobstructed. Old ladies with shopping bags, young ladies with prams were meandering freely up and down. What she didn't realize is that the law of obstruction says that one person standing still on the pavement is committing an offence. It's really a catch-all law designed to allow policemen to arrest whoever they want to – from the wideboy selling clockwork mice to the busker playing a penny whistle.

With the camera still turning, a black maria arrived. Much to the viewers' delight when the film was eventually broadcast, Esther automatically climbed in the wrong door, into the front of the black maria, and the policeman courteously climbed into the back, where prisoners normally go. She says her only excuse is that she's never done it before.

They drove to Fulham police station. There she sat next to a gentleman who had a heavy chain round his waist, two knives sticking out of his pocket and didn't look at all well. There was a great deal of muttering when the other policeman realized that all the senior staff seemed to be dealing with Esther, leaving the juniors to take a statement from the gentleman with the knives. But by then everyone seemed highly embarrassed and anxious to get rid of Esther as quickly as possible. They filled up a long form and she discovered that the policeman who arrested her was PC Herbert.

When they'd finished she put on her obliging smile and said:

'Shouldn't someone say to me that I'm not obliged to say anything but anything I do say will be taken down and may be used in evidence?'

The officer behind the desk cleared his throat and looked at PC Herbert. PC Herbert looked at the wall. No one had cautioned her. It's probable that people are hardly ever cautioned these days.

There was much excitement when Esther got back to the office. The BBC lawyers said she must go out that afternoon to finish the interviews otherwise she might create a precedent and admit defeat. When she arrived, outside Harrods this time, there were about fifty press photographers obstructing like mad – but no one seemed to care. They did their usual dirty trick persuading her to grimace horribly over the bat stew so that the next day the captions read 'Esther Aghast at her Arrest'. And cynics around the BBC decided, as cynics always do, that she'd done it all as a publicity stunt.

They were, of course, wrong. PC Herbert had absolutely no intention of luring more viewers to watch 'That's Life!'.

When the case eventually reached the magistrates' courts in Horseferry Road, half a dozen wideboys each charged with obstruction pleaded guilty before it was Esther's turn. One of them told her she was out of her mind to plead 'not guilty'.

'Plead guilty, apologize to the court. Pay half a nicker and you're out again,' he said.

As it turned out he was right. In spite of the fact that they showed their film in court, and the magistrate could see quite clearly that the pavement was extremely wide and the old ladies were trundling past, he still found Esther guilty of obstruction. She was fined £15.

She and the team have been out on street corners many times since but they've never met PC Herbert again. Certainly he added three million extra viewers to the 'That's Life!' audience.

*

When I was arrested it was more private – and much more painful. Mexico isn't the sort of place where you can rely on a sense of British fair play in the police force to protect you. We had stopped in El Paso, Texas for the night, making a 'Man Alive' documentary about the men who run the Holiday Inn chain. The crew suggested to the director, Adam Clapham, and me that we might all drive across the border a few miles away for a night out in Juarez. It would be dignified if I was able to report that I was reluctant to visit bars, and low-down vaudeville places, in a Mexican border town. It would be dignified – but untrue. I was among the first to jump into the station wagon.

After several beers, and several tequillas, in several bars, we were all recommended to a place on the outskirts of town where we were told exotic performances could be seen on stage. The barman who directed us there also assured us that the food was very good, even better than the ladies were pretty. That decided us. We went.

On our way home, driving back towards the American border, we were stopped by the Mexican police because the assistant cameraman, at the wheel, was travelling with only side lights, not the regulation dipped headlights. There were three policemen and they started to shout at the assistant cameraman, particularly when they found out that his driving licence was issued in Paris and was two years out of date.

Now, I may have been a little fuddled in my thinking at the time, but I remember recalling some advice I had been given, that when dealing with foreign policemen it was necessary to exhibit a great deal of authority, take command, be lordly. The assistant cameraman didn't speak Spanish and was getting confused. I did speak a little Spanish and so I decided that the time had come for me to rescue him and be lordly. Wrong.

I started by climbing out of the back of the car and clapping my hands very loudly to attract the attention of the Mexican police constables. I must admit that I surprised even myself with my hand clapping. There were three very sharp, loud reports, like pistol shots. The effect was beyond anything I might have imagined.

It seemed to rain policemen – on top of me. They came from doorways and other streets. Reinforcements arrived in cars. Within seconds, still struggling with my first lordly Spanish sentence of introduction, I was thrown into the back of a Mexican police car with all the windows and the space in front covered with chain link fencing, and two huge, garlic-smelling policemen piled in, one on each side of me. As the car started to accelerate away, Jim Peirson, the cameraman, shoved my passport into my hand through a small gap in the top of the chain link.

'I think you're going to need this Desi,' he said, with the awful prescience that has made him such a good cameraman and reliable friend.

The police car shot off into the night. As it drove away I tried my Spanish again. 'What a silly mistake this is. Let us now put it right,' I said carefully, taking out a packet of cigarettes and offering them to the uniformed gorillas alongside me. They both refused so I took one myself and lit it. I considered my next sentence.

The thug on my right leaned across and deliberately took the cigarette from my lips and stubbed it out in the centre of my cheek. I was promptly sick. All over his knees and shiny boots. His companion, on my left, then took advantage of the fact that I was leaning forward to pound me several times in the kidneys with the end of his truncheon.

A distinct sober chilliness was descending on me. It increased as I noticed that we'd just driven past the police station and were on our way out into the country. Beyond the edge of town we stopped. There in the darkness under a tree, still in the back seat of the car, the policeman whose uniform had suffered and his mate on the other side spent what seemed like hours, but was only a few minutes, 'working me over'. They pounded my rib cage and kidneys with their night sticks until I felt like a tenderized entrecôte steak. Later I discovered they'd broken four ribs but at the time I didn't care. During all this neither the two gorillas, nor the driver, spoke a word.

They drove me back to the police station where a smiling station sergeant told me I was to be charged with assault.

'We do not think you are drunk, señor, you will be pleased to hear. But if you make things difficult we would like to charge you with that as well,' he said.

Then they put me in the 'tank', a small grilled cage familiar to anyone who sees any of those detective movies.

When the sergeant returned and asked me if I would like to pay a 'fine' on the spot for assaulting his men, and save several nights in jail while they looked for a magistrate, I agreed at once. I didn't want any more trips to the edge of town.

'One hundred dollars,' he said and, as I reached for my wallet, 'We don't take traveller's cheques, señor.' I hadn't enough on me in cash. 'We thought you would not, señor, but your friends are waiting outside; maybe they would like to contribute.'

I started to become angry, always bad for clear thinking. This was nothing more than a 'shake-down' and there ought to be some way to get even. So I asked if I could have a receipt for the money, if my friends could find enough. That would be proof later.

'But of course, señor,' the sergeant told me, unperturbed.

Adam and the crew just managed to pool together a hundred dollars, a great deal of money then. The sergeant handed me my receipt.

'Oh, just one thing, señor,' he said. 'We have confiscated your car and all that filming equipment. If you wish to collect it, it is in the car park at the back of the police station. The man who is in charge will give it to you immediately. He will do that when you give him the receipt to prove that he was in order to release the car.'

Checkmate.

Back in El Paso, hours later, we were told I'd been comparatively lucky. The previous week an American air force colonel and his wife had been 'shaken down' for an invented traffic offence and the pair of them had been so badly beaten that they would need weeks in hospital.

When we flew on to the next city I was still mentally composing a letter to the British Ambassador in Mexico. I never did write the letter. Jim Peirson temporarily bandaged up my ribs with camera tape used for sealing film cans. By the time I got to a doctor in Memphis, to discover they were broken, I'd also come out in a rash. That's how I discovered I am allergic to camera tape. My night out in Juarez is one I'm not likely to forget easily.

We finished that film trip in the sedate tranquillity of Richmond, Virginia, at the headquarters of one of the American patriotic women's organizations. As we came out in the rain, a traffic warden was about to put a ticket on the windscreen of the camera car. I started to run towards it, trying to stop the ticket, saying, 'Don't do that ...'

I was overtaken by my young director, Adam Clapham. He threw both arms round me from behind and wrestled me to a halt.

'Oh my God, not again. I don't think I can bear it,' he said. 'Stay here. Stand still. Accept the ticket. How are your ribs feeling? ...'

6 Hospitality

The BBC regulation was clear, unequivocal – and intensely frustrating. Food eaten in hotel bedrooms was not to be charged on expenses. And that included breakfast, according to the bureaucratic bible of the BBC accountants. Food could only be consumed in hotel bedrooms if it was 'hospitality', that is entertaining, on behalf of the programme or the Corporation.

The lady researchers of 'Man Alive' had brought the problem to me, as their programme editor, in those days. All of them, and most of the men researchers too, preferred to have a cup of coffee, toast and orange juice in their hotel bedrooms when they were away on location.

But unless they went down to the dining room, where they could eat a full breakfast at twice the cost if they wanted, the regulations prevented them charging for anything in their rooms. Therefore, 'Catch 22' meant that a researcher, making phone calls to set up the day's filming while she had breakfast in her room, was expected to pay for the privilege of serving the BBC more efficiently. It didn't seem logical.

I authorized them all to write, on their hotel bills and expenses vouchers, next to the breakfast charge, the phrase 'entertaining in the bedroom'. Two weeks later the puritan morals of the BBC came into conflict – as I had hoped they would – with the stubborn bureaucracy of its administrative system. Puritanism won the day. The regulation was quietly changed. In future, they could have orange juice and toast in the bedroom, and charge it on expenses without offending Victorian morality.

'Hospitality' – drinks, a snack, or a slap-up four-course meal – is offered to people to persuade them to appear, then offered again just before they do and then afterwards, as though in celebration, when they have appeared. It's the excuse used by all those with expense accounts, from researchers to the Director-General, to pay for lunches and dinners in restaurants and hotels. Theoretically, staff in both the ITV companies and the BBC are not supposed to charge 'hospitality' for entertaining each other. In fact, it is what they most often do. A young film director who makes a camera crew stand for hours on a street corner in a snowstorm till he gets the shot he needs, has to unfreeze them with a comforting round or two of drinks, or they'll never work with him again. But that's an expensive round and he isn't paid enough to pay for it himself. So it goes down as 'Drinks to the Mayor of Penge'. There are, of course, armies of accountants whose job is to uncover these fictional mayors. How much simpler it would be if staff were allowed to tell the truth about their expenses – but much more boring too, without the game of cat and mouse with the accountants. And that is what leads to trouble.

David Attenborough remembers the time that he was filming in the remote villages of the South American pampas. In order to reach one particular tribe of rarely visited Indians he had to buy horses to carry him and the film crew, and packhorses for the equipment. They had to cross the wild, desolate 'Sea of Grass'. It was some days' ride.

When they arrived at the village, they filmed some remarkable sequences and the tribal Chief then offered to escort David and his crew a further two-day ride to the nearest road, where they could pick up some cars. The Chief and some of the elders went all the way to the waiting transport with David and the crew. When they parted, the tribesmen gave gifts to the men from the BBC. So, David Attenborough, in return for all their help in filming, gave them the horses, gifts from the great Corporation across the sea. The tribesmen accepted with quiet dignity.

Back home, David worked out his expenses and naturally included: 'To purchase of ponies and packhorses – £40'. But he'd forgotten the BBC accountants. Quick as a flash, they thought of a reason why he couldn't claim for horses on his expenses. 'Purchased goods or materials must remain the property of the Corporation and shall be delivered, by the claimant, to the Corporation. Therefore, we require not only a receipt but also the delivery up of the animals purchased, or an explanation for their absence . . .'

The qualities that make David Attenborough the success he is were present even in those early days. He didn't blow a fuse. Instead, he replied with a polite memo – but a short one.

'We ate them,' he wrote.

The BBC accountants remained silent, David's expenses were paid. One game to him.

Some unscrupulous players use tricks to beat accountants which neither of us admire and which certainly justify stern response from the bureaucrats. One producer we both know once ordered, at a restaurant, two more meals than there were people.

He then had the extra couple of expense account dinners wrapped up in 'doggy bags' so that he could take them home and put them in his deep freeze.

But conscience can also rise up in television executives. At a time of great economy in the BBC – and these days it always seems to be a time of great economy – the senior producers of the Current Affairs Group gathered for their weekly Friday lunch in one of the hospitality dining rooms in Lime Grove, Shepherd's Bush. It is a regular ritual with a serious purpose, a chance for the programme editors and producers to get together with other senior people and discuss staff and production problems. The meal, complete with wines and brandy, is prepared by the BBC catering service, 'hospitality' section. A high grade of lunch in the BBC catering system; not just cold cheese flan, but steaks in sauce, fruit, good cheese, all the trimmings.

On one Friday recently the table was littered with bottles, glasses and the remains of a good lunch. Several of the BBC's young 'Turks' were smoking cigars. The scene in the panelled room had the affluent atmosphere of a city boardroom, rather than the thrifty air of a public broadcasting organization. The waitress bustled out, leaving the door open to the corridor, which meant junior staff and technicians peeping in as they passed could see their bosses relaxing with port and stilton.

One senior producer at the lunch, more sensitive than the rest, was embarrassed by their comparative privilege and luxury. He said: 'Look, here we are cutting budgets, holding down wages, cancelling foreign trips, telling everybody how hard life is going to be and yet we sit at a table groaning with food and drink – and the door wide open to the world, for everyone to see. It's not really good enough and we ought to do something about it.'

His colleages all shouted at once: 'Shut the fucking door then!'

The smartest 'hospitality' party Esther and I ever remember attending on BBC premises was a farewell party for a wonderful BBC character, Mrs Lillian Reynolds, herself a hospitality waitress, who had served loyally for many years.

Now, whenever any of the big bosses at the BBC leave the Corporation, for reasons of old age, or gain promotion within the Corporation, or depart for any other reason (except when they're joining the opposition, in which case they're given two hours to clear out their desks and get off BBC premises) BBC parties are thrown. They usually take place in one of the canteens with a great many rather sad-looking vol-au-vents and sandwiches with curling edges accompanied by acidy white plonk or gritty red plonk. After all, everybody always consoles themselves, it's the spirit of the occasion that counts.

But when Lillian Reynolds finally retired, they threw

the party to end them all. Lily had been present at nearly every BBC hospitality occasion for more than two decades. There wasn't a Prime Minister, hardly a crowned head, certainly not an international star she hadn't served with a sausage on a stick and a glass or two of something to drink. So for her own party they all turned up. Michael Parkinson, Ned Sherrin, Huw Wheldon, every leading executive in the BBC and many in ITV, as well as half the politicians of the country. No one else in the BBC could have mustered such a guest list. What's more, it was the guests who wheeled in a piano and Cliff Morgan, the Head of Outside Broadcasts, responsible for royal occasions, who handed round song sheets and led us all in a specially rewritten version of 'Lily of Marlene' as a tribute to 'Lily of hospitality'.

Why this concentration on eating and drinking? It was designed in the beginning to overcome the panic of new interviewees by providing a drink before a programme which would numb inhibition, without paralysing the brain. It was later extended to include that 'mopping up' half hour after a programme when furious participants can be mollified, and presenters and their production teams can allow their racing adrenalin to calm down to normal level. 'Hospitality' then went on to become the label that was loosely attached to all entertainment charges in television. It covered everything from hiring a banqueting suite to launch a major new drama series, to buying a cup of tea for a helpful electrician in an outside organization. And also it became, naturally, the firm stamping ground of the men from accounts departments, each issued with an abacus and a rule book. That made it a series of diplomatic tightropes for television executives to walk behind the scenes.

For instance, how do you stop a well-known Tory politician from consuming six glasses of Scotch, before his appearance, instead of a single glass of wine? If he then weaves around in front of camera in that way that scores of press officers have now learned to explain as 'fatigued and emotional', should you stop him? The answer is you can't.

I once tried, with the co-operation of a great man's permanent under-secretary. It resulted in a sound rocketing for both of us from the great man himself, who then stamped over to the small bar in the hospitality room, poured himself one of the largest whiskies I've ever seen, swallowed it at a gulp, refilled it and, glaring at us like a prep school boy finally getting his own way, marched towards the studio holding the equivalent of four large drinks in one glass.

Half an hour later he calmly shot holes in his own cabinet policy without appearing to notice, he also laid all blame for all the problems on the opposition, avoided directly answering any question put to him – and smugly finished the whisky. He thought he'd done well. Everybody else thought he'd been a disaster. His permanent under-secretary blamed me and I blamed the permanent under-secretary. If there ever was an inquest at Number 10 Downing Street, after the broadcast – and it was the sort of occasion that might well have produced one – then I'm sure the great man blamed us, the broadcasters. He always had in the past, and now was no time for him to change his pattern.

In the early days of BBC programmes, a rather stern secretarial lady was employed by the hospitality section of the catering division to keep an iron grip on the drinks cabinet to prevent just such an occasion. But she couldn't be everywhere at once, and most viewers remember only too well the occasions when her grip failed – they've seen the results on the screen.

'Hospitality' also extends to the kind of party that is usually thrown at the end of a successful series. That's when everybody is expected to let their hair down – and not tell tales about it afterwards. And usually, in the case of a successful programme series, the bosses don't look too closely at the hospitality charge on the budget of the final programme.

For some years 'That's Life!' held its end-of-series party in a Bayswater hotel which had a heated indoor swimming pool attached to the banqueting room. Eventually, old timers learned not to come in their best clothes, also to bring a towel, even a swimming costume. When the hotel management, after years of loyal custom from the programme, decided that it was a rather noisy and down-market occasion the imaginative production team hired two narrow boats on the Regents Park Canal, lashed side by side.

Traditionally such parties are always attended by the big bosses, so when I escorted the Controller of BBC-1 up the gangplank he looked suitably flattered to be greeted by two highly exotic professional 'hostesses' in sequinned long dresses, heavy make-up and much jewellery. He looked a little astonished when they both insisted on giving him smacking great kisses for the benefit of the team's photographer. But he kept his composure well, until I revealed that the attractive ladies were two young male researchers on the team who had decided to celebrate 'in drag'. The Controller spent some time that evening extracting a promise from me that I would get hold of the negatives. I failed.

Sometimes it's the star of a series or show who throws a party – David Frost never failed to make headlines with his. Breakfast for Prime Ministers at a London hotel, or the time he took over Battersea Funfair. At a party at the end of a quiz series, one of this country's best known comics invited a local Chinese restaurant to provide the food. We discovered that they were also cooking it on the premises. The ladies loo in the basement of the BBC Television Centre had three primus stoves burning away with simmering cauldrons of Chinese specialities on top. There was so much smoke I was surprised the automatic sprinklers weren't triggered off. But the comedian in question is an old hand at long series – and the parties at the end of them. It would take a great deal to ruffle his composure.

I remember another end-of-series party thrown by a production team in Glasgow when they had completed a series of six documentary dramas in which those famous television detectives, Barlow and Watt from 'Softly, Softly', looked at classic unsolved murder cases from history. The Glasgow authorities had been most co-operative, and the production team very properly invited the Chief of Police as one of the guests to the party at the end of the series.

David McNee was even then nicknamed 'Hammer'

McNee by both the police and criminals of Glasgow. He was about to be appointed Commissioner of the Metropolitan Police at New Scotland Yard and receive his knighthood. He arrived at the party in the full splendour of his Chief Constable's uniform. He is a formal and dignified man and the world of television must sometimes seem to him a rather sloppy, undisciplined place. If he had any doubts about that, they were clearly resolved when the man who had been responsible for all the costumes in the series swayed towards him, draped an arm round his uniformed shoulder, pouted at him affectionately and said:

'Hello, I'm in ladies' frocks.'

The Chief Constable of Glasgow didn't stay long at the party.

Mind you, Solzhenitsyn, when I asked him to lunch at the BBC in order to discuss a film proposal, arrived late because he'd insisted on travelling by tube train and then changed his mind, once he'd entered the Television Centre, on the grounds that it would be a moral betrayal of his principles to eat a capitalist meal on capitalist premises. He absolutely refused to stay to lunch so we dolefully sat down to eat the meal by ourselves – minus the guest of honour. Later Solzhenitsyn went to live in America, where he has not – as far as I can tell – abandoned all the good things of life in the world's most thriving example of capitalist endeavour.

Ernest Marples, the bouncing and energetic Conservative cabinet minister, grew to understand the nature of television hospitality, both ITV and BBC, so well that he finally couldn't bear it any longer. Mainly, he couldn't bear the quality of wine we served. Mr Marples was more than a wine connoisseur, he owned a vineyard. At a time when, as Minister of Transport, he frequently arrived for television interviews on a bicycle, he would bring with him, in the basket on the handlebars, a bottle of one of his own vintages. He would then supervise the drawing of the cork with care, inspect the glass for cleanliness and apologize charmingly for not offering anybody else a drink because, as he rightly explained, 'there wouldn't be enough to go round – and I really can't stand the stuff that you provide but it doesn't seem to damage any of you.'

It's always intriguing to find out how other organizations deal with 'hospitality'. I discovered that it's even a problem which can worry the President of the United States. When I was filming 'The First Lady', a profile of Rosalyn Carter, for the 'Americans' series, we flew on one of the presidential jets, with Mrs Carter, to Puerto Rico. At 35,000 feet we interviewed her about her life as First Lady. The journey was a short one and the dozen or so reporters also on the plane were, like us, offered Coca Cola, soft drinks, tea or coffee – and peanuts, served by the Air Force Master Sergeant in charge of the cabin staff.

Just after the plane had landed and was taxiing towards the welcoming crowds and the waiting band, the Master Sergeant went round the reporters and photographers – and us, the BBC crew. 'Did you have peanuts with your complimentary drink?' he asked. And if you'd eaten the peanuts you paid forty cents, if you'd had two bowls, eighty cents.

When I joked later with the First Lady about a President who started life as a peanut farmer charging for them on the presidential plane, she laughed.

'At first I used to be embarrassed myself,' she told me. 'But it's all part of Jimmy's drive to cut down on the free hospitality and you have to make the rule apply everywhere if you want to gain respect for practising economies – and that even includes the peanuts on President Carter's airplanes.'

At least, I reflected, back home in the BBC the peanuts are free.

7 Commercial break

I was on location in Wiltshire on the banks of what was meant
to be a mountain stream. They were making a cigarette
commercial, in the days when cigarettes were still legally
allowed to be advertised on the screen. The image they wished
to create was that smoking one of their cigarettes, stuffed as it
was with the products of the eucalyptus and the menthol
bush, would produce a 'cool' sensation. Frankly, the damned
things made me dizzy but I was there to observe the
commercial, not pass judgement on the product.

Coming, as I did, from the world of documentary and
current affairs film makers where, in those days, a team of
more than six or seven people was huge – I was bowled over
with what was going on. There were more than fifty people on
location. Every hotel in the area had been booked completely
for a week. The vehicles needed to carry the technicians, the
cast, the props, costumes, make-up and equipment caused
unheard of traffic jams in quiet Wiltshire lanes. Dinner and
drinks in the evening seemed more like a never ending series of
goodbye parties, or retirement celebrations, than the
necessary feeding of a film crew at work.

At the centre of this razzmatazz convention were the men
from the advertising agency. Grey-flannel-suited and floral-

tied to a man, they dominated the proceedings. They strode everywhere clasping their bibles, the 'storyboards', which dictated every detail of the commercial, each one showing precisely what was expected from the highly talented cameraman, director and other technicians - a series of little cartoon drawings, exactly like a comic, totally preventing any of these well paid artists doing anything creative.

But the best laid storyboards 'gang aft agley'. After four days, the location hit a crisis. The plot called for a young man to swing down a hillside, between the silver birch trees, holding hands with a pretty girl, bend down to pick a primrose from the bank of the mountain stream and then gaze fondly at the girl, before launching the primrose into the stream where the camera would follow it as it floated away. Later the cigarette package would be superimposed, and they would add the 'Cool' lullaby. Very artistic.

They had the man, the girl, the silver birch trees and, with a little careful damming higher up, the bubbling mountain stream. They had also carefully planted out-of-season primroses. But still it was all going wrong.

Primroses, it turned out, don't float. The young man did his stuff, again and again; the young girl smiled into his eyes, as he picked the flowers we'd planted so carefully and chucked them into the water. They sank.

Forty highly-paid expert artists struggled to achieve the effect dictated for them on the storyboard. Nature defeated all of them.

Eventually, one night after about the fifteenth or sixteenth bottle of Niersteiner had been finished, one of the young men from the agency proved his right to a grey flannel suit and a footnote in the history of Madison Avenue and Curzon Street. 'Plastic primroses. Foam primroses,' he said.

There was the kind of silence that must have followed the discovery of the world's great inventions, the wheel, gravity, even fire. Sketches were made, specifications discussed, technicians were drawn into the argument. The melting temperature of paint was discussed, the reflectability of foam rubber, sliced thin, was debated. Phone calls were made to London.

For three days all of us waited – not without food and drink, and with each other for entertainment – in the Wiltshire countryside while a firm in Stepney which made flowery summer hats laboured and sweated on the primroses. Finally, in the panniers of four motorcycles, they were rushed to the mountain stream. Plastic primroses, thousands of them, ready to be skewered into position in the centre of real primrose leaves.

They worked. They floated like a dream in take after take. They young man smiled, the young girl dimpled – and the primroses, one by one, floated away downstream. All of them. Nobody was content until every single primrose had been used.

For years afterwards, as I watched the result on our TV screen, I wondered if fishermen at sea had ever been puzzled on stormy nights, when they hauled aboard a net full of struggling cod and ling and whiting – and found in the middle of it a plastic primrose or two. Now perhaps they know the answer.

Of course, there are very strict rules about what advertisers can or cannot say in commercials. The Independent Broadcasting Authority, the IBA, has firm views about taste, for instance. False teeth cannot be shown on television – those cleansing tablets have to be dropped into a glass full of large plastic letters spelling their brand name. Armpits, smooth or hairy, are ruled to be offensive. So deodorants can't roll over them. You can't look down into a loo when you're filming it with something that kills every known germ, but for some reason you are allowed to put your camera into the loo and then look out.

Apart from taste, there are also rules about honesty. If you are doing a comparison test, washing one shirt in one powder and one in another, you have to convince the IBA that your test results are completely fair. But once they have agreed the script, they very rarely, if ever, visit the film location and watch how the directors film it. And that is where the cheating goes on.

Take those ladies in shampoo advertisements, swinging their perfect glossy golden hair. Seldom, if ever, have they really washed it in the shampoo they're advertising. We revealed, on 'That's Life!', that the hairstyles used to demonstrate a miracle new kind of curling tong had, in fact, been created with old fashioned heated rollers. Why? Because the model is picked for her pretty hair, and the hairdresser is chosen because he can make glamorous styles, quickly and professionally in studio conditions, under hot lights, with a desperately short deadline. And hairdressers are prima donnas, like cooks and gardeners, they insist on using the equipment they trust, know and have come to rely on. Also, because the film directors have long ago forgotten that the viewers are looking at the commercial to see if the new shampoo really does live up to its claims, they don't care what shampoo is really used. They probably don't even ask.

The one person who is never consulted is the manufacturer, the client. He'll be kept firmly away until the finished commercial is edited and dubbed with seductive music and persuasive commentary. If cheating goes on he is as likely to be conned as the viewer. If the directors cared about the truth of their films they could easily ask the manufacturer to supply his own hairdresser, someone who is prepared to use the real shampoo. But it never seems to happen.

More excusable are the food cheats. It is very difficult to photograph food under those burning studio lights without it melting or wilting. Ice cream is almost impossible. The film-makers have often used mashed potato instead. The head on a pint of beer will never foam long enough to give time for the cameraman to practise a shot, or rehearse a pretty barmaid. The 'props' man swishes washing up liquid into it. What the viewer – and the client – doesn't see, the IBA can't grieve over.

There was panic in one advertising agency when the manufacturer of a sparkling wine dropped in to see his latest

PUSSY WALKS IN.

PUSSY SEES BEEFOES!

PUSSY SNIFFS BEEFOES!!

PUSSY HATES BEEFOES!!!

PUSSY WALKS OFF !!!!

GET ANOTHER DAMN PUSSY.

commercial. Someone had forgotten to edit the end of the film. So, after the camera zoomed in to those delicious bubbles winking at the brim of the glass, and held it there for the final moments, instead of a slow fade a hairy hand came into shot and squirted in another slug of Schh, you know who's soda water. The client stormed out – it was hours before they could calm him down enough to explain that the genuine bubbles were beautiful, but somehow didn't show up quite as well as soda water.

It's taken for granted that the way to make a wooden table really gleam in a commercial for furniture polish is to cover it with a sheet of glass. Those sizzling sausages in the frying pan in one commercial have been carefully painted with brown nail polish to make them look appetizing. Stews and casseroles get a coat of varnish.

In a recent commercial for bubble bath the bubbles had all burst by the end of the first rehearsal, leaving the model's top half bare and goose-pimpled. Once again, the props man came to the rescue with another chemical from his 'cheat kit'. This time the bubbles lasted. Finally the model climbed thankfully out of the bath and, reaching for a towel, found she was covered with blue blotches. The chemical was great for maintaining foam under the lights but not so wonderful for skin.

Perhaps the biggest surprise about commercials is how much time, attention, talent and money is spent on a thirty-second advertisement. Top actors earn a fortune from adding their voices – Orson Welles, Richard Briars, Penelope Keith. And sometimes inspired casting for a commercial will create a genuine new comedy team – Joan Collins and Leonard Rossiter are a perfect example. Their Cinzano advertisement is also another example of an IBA rule. No advertisement for drink is allowed to imply that one sip will lead to romance, or greater virility, or heightened sex appeal. So Rossiter had to be cast as a clown who drowns Joan Collins in lumps of ice. And in half a minute they created a delightful sketch, and a running series that has now become part of the comedy tradition of this country.

Many of the commercials these days are directed by the most creative directors in the industry. It has become accepted that they are the new generation of feature film directors. The top directing names always did make commercials. Now the brightest of the new names are as likely to be used.

A commercial is an opportunity for talented film makers to stretch themselves, to call for exotic locations or inventive shots. More money will be pumped into a sixty-second commercial than goes into the budget of a television play. The results are often such stylish and beautiful commercials that they completely outclass the programmes they interrupt. (And of course jingles have become the new nursery rhymes, every toddler sings them along with the television set.)

When non-actors – 'civilians' – appear in commercials it's usually because the advertiser is paying highly for the integrity of the person being used to endorse his product. Alan Whicker and David Frost, as well known international travellers, have both been paid highly to endorse different airlines. And Sir Robert Mark, when he retired, was paid £100,000 for making a commercial supporting the claims of a tyre manufacturer. He gave all that he earned from that to charity, which effectively stifled critics and gossips and was a gesture that we found admirable.

But because of the deep doubting instinct in viewers when they are being 'sold' something, people like Esther and Sir Robin Day have never made a commercial. If you earn your living on the basis of independent investigative journalism, however careful you are only to endorse the truth, a commercial may damage your standing as a 'Consumer Queen' or a political inquisitor. So – for the time being – you won't be hearing certain voices during the commercial breaks. A pity really. Just think what Robin Day could do for bow-ties, horn-rimmed specs, or cigars.

8 Men versus Women

This chapter is really about women and pigs – Male Chauvinist Pigs. It's also about love and sex – the first is frowned on, the second takes place, but where it takes place mustn't embarrass television bosses.

But let's start with a woman's place. And, wherever that ought to be, there was a time when there was one place women were never going to be, the most sacred place in the BBC and ITV – the newsroom.

Women can't read the news. That's that. For years there was no argument, no doubt. It was firmly believed by both ITV and BBC bosses that a woman reading the news would distract the viewers from the events she was reporting, because of her feminine personality. They said that women's voices didn't have the same timbre as men's when it came to dealing with emergencies and national disasters, they even said they were frightened that, when 'newsreading' disaster stories, women would burst into tears.

It may seem difficult to believe all this in the age of Angela Rippon, Anna Ford and Jan Leeming but, remember, television used to be almost exclusively the business of men. In many areas it still is. And even in the areas where there has been an emancipated breakthrough, the relationship between women and their male television colleagues is still edgy, uncomfortable and quarrelsome. Men versus women. There is still great management antipathy towards women, towards employing them, promoting them, trusting them – or putting them in charge. It isn't, you can bet, an antipathy that applies when it comes to rattling bedroom doorknobs in hotel corridors on location, or asking for sympathy and understanding over dinner for two (and asking for even more than sympathy after that). Sex, it seems, in television circles is meant to be liberal even if women are not to be liberated.

It is often believed that men won't work for a woman boss. Why anybody still bothers to advance the argument when the short history of television management and production is peppered with the names of significant women producers and executives is beyond us. But the BBC's Current Affairs department was moulded and shaped by the indomitable Mrs Grace Wyndham-Goldie. And her 'young men' of those days included Donald Baverstock, Alasdair Milne, Huw Wheldon, Ned Sherrin, David Attenborough, Michael Peacock, Paul Fox and many others; all of whom have gone on to distinguished careers and top jobs in television. All of whom, also, still speak in awe of the lady boss described by one senior executive as having 'a whim of iron'.

There was Mrs Joanna Spicer, a top BBC executive who, among other things, gave Esther her first job in television and made it her task, among the almost exclusively male ranks of senior executives, to seek out, and bring forward, talented women in television production. Monica Simms ran BBC Children's Programmes for many successful years and is now the Controller of Radio Four. Director Jenny Barraclough has no difficulty in engaging the loyalty of all the men who work with her, and for her. Yvonne Littlewood's name as producer at the end of the credits on a Light Entertainment production is a hallmark of quality. Esther herself has for the past nine years, not only written and presented 'That's Life!' but also produced it, with male directors, researchers and reporters happily on the team. But still the myth about women persists. For many years I attended BBC Television's most important weekly meeting of executives, **Programme Review Board**. There would usually be about thirty heads of departments at the meeting. It was a rare day if there were two women departmental heads among them and frequently, most recently, there would be no women present at all.

'But women go off and have babies and interrupt their career paths, that's why they never reach executive level,' we are always told. But you will never be told that by the women who have successfully combined motherhood and work – it comes from men, men who combined fatherhood and work – and also made it to the top.

One evening Esther and her executive producer, a man, joined me and my boss for a drink in the office. My boss was a large and energetic man who has since risen to an even more important position in the BBC. He was holding forth about some problem of television politics – he was very good at television politics. He also knew a great deal of what went on in the highest echelons of the BBC. He was, therefore, fascinating to listen to on the subject. He lowered his voice and even glanced over his shoulder as men do when delivering a really confidential piece of gossip. 'Gentlemen, between the three of us,' he began. There were four people in the room, three men – and one woman. Mind you, I've been guilty of precisely the same kind of patronizing assumptions myself. John Lloyd once pointed out to me that I only started paying real attention to the acting performances of the curvaceous Hilary Pritchard, in 'Braden's Week', after somebody had told me that she spoke Russian and was highly qualified academically. John Lloyd had a theory that it was an inverted form of sexism to be 'turned on' by a high IQ.

He felt, also, that I was the best example of it he could ever find.

I gazed at Miss Pritchard on the monitor screen in the control room, where we were, as John continued to expound his theory. There was a lot of Hilary on the screen. Speaking technically she had become the focus of everybody's attention. The question was: would the top of her dress stay up? Nobody else seemed to care whether she spoke Russian.

I sighed. Being a male supporter of women's liberation can sometimes be a lonely business.

What's more, there are plenty of women who will not hesitate to use that ancient weapon, feminine wiles, to achieve their aim. They may be betraying the liberation – but they're also demonstrating masculine gullibility – and vanity. I was sitting in my office at the BBC once, when a beautiful lady reporter, who has since gone on to become a television star, wandered in and asked if she could look through my bookshelf for something to read during a flight to Belfast, where she was headed with a 'Man Alive' film team. I waved cheerfully towards the books on the wall.

She browsed for some minutes and eventually selected one I had written myself. 'I've never read this and I've often wanted to,' she said, her large shining eyes gazing at me. 'I so admire anybody who writes a book at all, and particularly on a difficult subject like this. Do you mind if I borrow it for the journey?' I was, of course, flattered by her choice and happily muttered something grateful as she wandered from the room with the book. Out of more than a thousand books on the shelves, *my* book.

I spent the rest of the day in a mild state of euphoria, flattered out of all proportion by the gesture, as I dealt with a succession of tedious administrative demands. When Esther wandered in, later that evening, to see if I'd finished work and could give her a lift home I couldn't help preening myself.

'So,' I finished the story, 'she's gone off with my book to read. And don't give me that cynical look, it was a perfectly genuine gesture. That is a very intelligent girl who wanted to read my book.'

We were interrupted as my secretary, the ever-smiling, blonde Cheryl, trotted in to tidy up the office for the night. She went straight to the bookshelves and replaced in the shelves the book that had so recently – and so flatteringly – been borrowed. It had travelled no further than the coffee table in the office outside.

The silence in the car as I drove Esther home that night was thick with the intolerable smugness of a woman who has been proved right about the effect of feminine flattery on masculine vanity.

Anyway, I comforted myself, nobody calls Mrs Thatcher a 'cop out' on women's lib because she insisted on a flower arrangement as part of the set 'dressing' when she was being interviewed on programmes like 'Panorama'. It was a demand discussed by a meeting of the highest level of BBC executives before it was, finally, agreed to. At the time, Jim Callaghan was Leader of the Opposition and I was not applauded, at that meeting, for suggesting that he ought to be offered a reciprocal political arrangement – a kind of Constance Spry 'right of reply'. Or if he preferred, I suggested, a variation on a theme – how about a Harvest Festival arrangement of fruit and vegetables, including turnips, marrows, ears of corn ... I could have developed my theme, but I was shouted down.

But it's not all war between men and women. Inside and outside working hours it often becomes a warmer relationship – so the television companies have created rules to keep sex if not out of mind, at least out of sight.

When, with Bill Morton my partner, I first joined the BBC as a programme editor in 1965, I arrived pink with energy, bustling with ideas, anxious to brief our new team of researchers, directors and reporters, for this invention, 'Man Alive'. Instead, I was confronted by two men in the kind of brown coat favoured by Ronnie Barker in comedy sketches. The fact that one of them was taller, like Ronnie Barker, and the other was short and bespectacled, made it almost impossible for me to concentrate on their very serious purpose. They had brought swathes of material and fabric pattern books. It turned out I had joined the ranks of BBC executive management and it would be impossible for me to serve the Corporation properly until I'd chosen the office curtains.

'Non-draw' of course. 'You're not senior enough yet for full-draw curtains,' said the Ronnie Barker man. 'Non-draw' curtains, he explained, were only eighteen inches wide and hung purely to decorate the sides of the windows, not to stop the light or to prevent people looking in. Why? – 'We believe it's all down to Lord Reith and the time when he was Director-General. He was quite sure that there'd be goings-on on the office carpet. So, he thought, as long as he could stop them drawing the curtains he'd keep the Corporation pure.'

Later that week they returned and fitted my 'non-draw' curtains. I noticed that, non-draw or not, the two Ronnies of the BBC curtain division were busy hammering and screwing a full-length curtain track into position.

'Isn't that an awful waste of money when all we are supplied with is these fringe curtains?' I asked.

The Ronnie Barker one replied 'Well, you see, a young executive like you is likely to go further up the ladder and then you would be entitled to full-draw curtains. So then we don't have to go to the bother of changing the pelmet and track when you get your promotion. Which, no doubt, will be very soon – and no more than you deserve,' he added kindly.

'But what about all those Reithian principles and the protection of the Corporation morality?' I asked.

'Ah, the Corporation reckons that when you're promoted you won't need to try it on the office carpet, because you'll either be able to afford a nice hotel – or you'll be too old to want to.'

But it was the bosses of one ITV company, a small but highly reputable station, who received their puritanical nemesis in the most embarrassing circumstances. The Controller of Programmes was a strict, authoritarian man and untidy things, like sex, drink, sometimes even laughter, may have had their place, but it certainly wasn't in his television station. He used to boast to visiting parties of MPs, VIPs and business men that he knew everything that was going on, every minute of the day. To prove his point, their conducted tour would finish in his office where one wall consisted of a bank of television monitors, their screens blank.

He would then explain that, from his desk, he could 'lock in' to any of the machines in the station, and watch the progress of a play, a current affairs programme, an afternoon movie, or religious programme.

He pressed buttons. Screens lit up. His point was proved - and sherry would be served. On one tour, he finished his speech – and started pressing buttons. Every single one of the fourteen television monitors banked against the wall of his office came alight. Each and every one was showing the same scene from 'Deep Throat'. Desperately he pressed more buttons. 'Deep Throat' continued to show. Every video tape engineer was busy recording pirate copies of the Linda Lovelace pornographic spectacular.

To my distress, history does not record what explanation the Controller of Programmes made. It's said that several members of the party were anxious that he shouldn't switch off the screens. It is also true that, shortly after the VIPs had departed, several senior members of the station's technical staff left for good. It turned out they had been running a thriving business, transferring blue movies to video tape.

In another ITV company in London I was actually present when the management discovered that the early morning cleaning ladies were turning up even earlier than their normal four a.m. start in order to 'star' in blue movies, which were being filmed by cameramen and film editors using the studio sets for children's programmes and the grey tweed sofa in the Managing Director's office.

It seemed the 'Mrs Mop' brigade would arrive, long before dawn, made up to the nines, dressed in sequins and glitter ready for the kind of performances which certainly would never be seen on television. Volunteer film editors also played starring roles.

Filming over, the ladies would parcel up their fish-net stockings and frothy dresses, shove curlers back in their hair, scarves round their heads, put thick skirts and aprons back on – and set about cleaning offices and corridors.

The discovery of their activities led to a huge dilemma at the highest level of management. Morally speaking, the ladies, and the film editors, should be dismissed. But office cleaners were impossible to recruit, and good film editors were hard to find. Expediency ruled the day. The film editors were chastened and the Mrs Mops were chastised. Children's programmes continued to appear on the screen, the offices remained clean, the Managing Director's sofa went back to its boring life of receiving only the weight of executive behinds – and I like to think the Mrs Mops found some other form of 'moonlighting' – or perhaps some other place for the same kind.

But the worst crime of all, it seems, isn't sex – it's love.

Falling in love may be wonderful when it's happening on the TV screens to Doris Day or Judy Garland, surrounded by bluebirds and accompanied by all those singing violins. But when it happens to the real live people of television, it confuses the bosses, alarms the shareholders, disturbs the creaking emotions of Boards of Governors and produces scandal in the papers.

If Fred loves Sue, and Desmond loves Esther, and they work together – then there's a problem to worry about. Is it fair? Will they influence each other at work? You can take your secretary out to dinner, or a weekend in Amsterdam, even fiddle the cost on your expenses; you can have an affair with a colleague, meet secretly in little pubs and darkened car parks – that's all part of life's rich and varied pattern. But if you fall in love, let the world know, get married, drive home together openly, come to work in the same car – then that's a crime.

The secretive whispers of an affair can even be an accepted thing. But ordinary domestic conversation over the breakfast table, or together in the evening, is somehow seen as a threat. They are frightened that you may be discussing work, talking about colleagues, arguing about programme ideas, planning new and better ways to make television. After all, if you're not having a secret affair it's quite likely that you will have time to talk about work, it may even be that your shared enjoyment of work is what brought you together in the first place. And it's almost certain that your television employers are benefiting from the extra time and mental energy that the pair of you are giving to your work. But 'pillow talk' is probably the most feared disease in television. It shouldn't be, it is our belief that very little of commercial, artistic, political or broadcasting significance is ever said on the pillow. I always did think that all those spies operating in the Mata Hari mould were probably giving rather more than they received, but I expect they went on with it because they enjoyed their work. In fact, it is the bitchy gossip of men in clubs and pubs, round the canteen table, or over the expense account lunch which is more likely to produce the unjust assessments, the unkind labels, and the unfair promotions and sackings. That doesn't matter. It is married couples working together that are seen as a threat. For the sake of their own identities, it's probably best for them to work apart while television organizations still allow (even encourage) destructive gossip and back-stabbing methods of gaining promotion.

We have yet to meet a husband and wife team working in television who have, because of their marriage, seriously damaged or affected the careers of those for whom they were responsible in professional terms. But human nature is, I fear, inclined to believe in nepotism and favouritism.

For years I went to some trouble to ensure that the department I ran for the BBC was heavily staffed with talented women, whose company I have always enjoyed. I saw to it that all the women were encouraged, if they wished, to marry, have babies and still keep right on working. Director Jenny Barraclough had all four of her children at intervals between making award-winning 'Man Alive' programmes and documentary films, all over the world. For some time, I even encouraged a redoubtable Scottish lady, in charge of all our audio typing, to use the stationery store room as an illicit crèche for her own children and any other 'bairns' belonging to her small army of lady typists. I, personally, got huge satisfaction out of my meetings with the children – and earned myself the label 'baby freak'. Rather smugly I used to think that I was also earning a place in heaven and, perhaps, even a niche in some footnote of emancipist history. Wrong.

Some of those same ladies were among the first to criticize the fact that Esther and I worked together in the same department.

Mind you, married ladies in television have a lot to put up with. No wonder they sometimes do go mad. It's often the wives of middle-aged men who suspect that their husbands are up to no good when they stay late at the office. Usually they're right.

One admirable and energetic wife of a rather distinguished producer finally became so convinced that her husband Timothy was having an affair with his secretary that she discovered the poor girl's address, and arrived there late one night – having left the children with a neighbour – clutching a carving knife. She discovered the couple in that most damning of all *in flagrante* positions – sitting side-by-side on the sofa watching television, not even holding hands, a truly hurtful picture of domestic extra-marital bliss.

Fortunately for everybody the wife had telephoned one of the reporters on the team during the earlier part of her search for her husband and the reporter, knowing the truth of the affair, had driven as fast as he could to the secretary's flat – just in time to grab the carving knife and then administer large glasses of brandy to the weeping wife, the terrified secretary and the cowering husband.

But it didn't end there. Husband Timothy announced that he was in love. He didn't go home on the domestic lead. He stayed where he was. The next day, Mrs Timothy came roaring down the BBC corridors, opening door after door and shrieking at the horrified occupants 'Where is he? I know you're hiding him, I'm going to kill the bastard. He's just a menopausal Romeo, and you wait till I tell her a few home truths about him.'

By the time she reached my office door, I'd been warned – but there was no bolt. I was defenceless and I came in for an extra barrage or two. It was all my fault. I was to blame. I was the sex-mad idiot that had brought all these women into the department in the first place. My turn would come and I'd be sorry. (It did and I was – but that's another story.)

Two doors further down the corridor, she found her husband. His secretary was already locked in the Ladies and he was trying to crawl into the knee hole of his desk. She started throwing things. The noise was fearful, particularly when his heavy glass ashtray shattered a plate glass window. Even then, not one of us had the courage to interfere. The building was emptying fast as producers, researchers and reporters discovered urgent assignments elsewhere. In the end the poor lady grew tired, naturally enough, and her husband took her home.

He's married to the secretary now, and his ex-wife is very happy and calm – and also, I'm glad to say, gets the giggles when she remembers the day she started throwing ashtrays.

There is another kind of loving madness that overtakes ladies in television, the organization spinster syndrome. Usually it's the result of too much devotion to work and sometimes too much devotion to drinking and gossiping with colleagues, after work. It's no respecter of age or seniority. I've seen it in secretaries in their twenties and still be vigorously present in lady executives approaching retirement in their sixties. One girlfriend of Esther's who worked for me stands out in our memory. They'd been together as colleagues since their early days as researchers on '24 Hours'. Samantha was a tweedy lady – put her in the staff common room of a minor girls' public school and, with her neat bobbed hair, and sensible shoes, she would fit in perfectly. But beneath her county exterior, there boiled a passionate temperament, a latin madness which occasionally exploded. The first time we were aware of its volcanic potential was one Valentine's Day.

The head of BBC Personnel was a friendly, extraordinarily well-bred gentleman, passionate about rose-growing, courteous to everybody, particularly ladies. He would hold doors open for them, manoeuvre so that he walked on the outside of the pavement, and maintained a scrupulously polite and formal relationship with his two secretaries.

On the morning that he rang me, he was almost inarticulate with rage. 'Your Samantha,' he exploded. (Why is it that when staff, colleagues, or even children, have done anything wrong, they immediately become 'yours' rather than 'ours'?)

'What's wrong now?' I said in some astonishment, because I'd never seen him even irritable, let alone in a rage.

'That girl has sent me a Valentine – a hideous great thing with a red satin heart in the middle of it, and pink and green ribbons all round it,' he said.

'Well, I admit it's unusual, and probably in rather bad taste, but it's a nice enough gesture really – anyway, how do you know it's from her? Valentines are supposed to be anonymous,' I replied.

'She's signed the flaming thing.'

'I knew she was discontented with her job, and actually I thought she was inclined – quite unfairly of course – to blame you,' I said. 'I think we should both be pleased that she's made this friendly gesture – even if it is a little eccentric.'

'Eccentric my arse,' he said, shocking me into silence. I'd never even heard him say 'damn' before. 'You don't know what she said on it. It was opened by my secretary and both of the girls in my office have read it now. I don't know how I can look them in the face again. That girl has ruined my life. She's got to go.'

'But what's she said?'

'I don't want to tell you.'

'How can I help you if you won't tell me?'

A pause. 'All right then. It says: "You've been screwing me for years and I think it's time we let the whole world know about it, don't you?" signed Samantha. And just in case there's any confusion she's put her surname, her room number and telephone extension on the thing!'

I managed to calm him. He really was a very nice person, and had done nothing to deserve the disturbance and shock which had suddenly entered his quiet, rose-growing middle years. He agreed in the end that if Samantha was given a stern rocketing by David Attenborough, his boss and mine, it would serve the purpose. He would not accept less than that. He was also a very formal man and a strict adherent to the rules. I often felt that the wonderful roses he grew in his Surrey garden were probably too frightened to do anything else but bloom on time. And that should have been the end of it. But it wasn't.

I sent for Samantha and she explained, with open-faced candour, that it had become her mission to 'de-stuff' the senior members of the hierarchy. It was, she had decided, the only way to introduce humanity back into a system which had become stiff and unfeeling.

'Well, you've done that now, and enough is enough,' I suggested. 'I'm afraid you will have to take your rocketing, but that's the price of practical joking.'

'Oh, but I wasn't joking – and I haven't finished,' she said, more wide-eyed than ever.

We let it go at that. I was convinced that it was all over and we'd saved the day. Wrong again.

Two days later I received a stencilled copy of a five page memo written by Samantha to the Director-General of the BBC, on the subject of the Head of Personnel's character and behaviour. It amounted to a kind of 'annual report', written on the Corporation's very own dignified rose-growing gentleman. It was fascinating – and terrifying. Among other things, it assessed him as a sex symbol. It meandered off into the description of an affair she had once had with another man, who'd risen to a position of great importance in the BBC (I personally couldn't help being fascinated by her description of their nights together and her suggestion that he was shaped rather like an amorous rugby ball.)

Then I remembered, the real time bomb was ticking threateningly away in the top left hand corner of the first page of her ludicrous, meandering, sexy madnesses. She had copied the memo to nearly every senior executive in the Corporation, including David Attenborough, as the Director of Programmes, and many other top men whose personal lives she appeared to be describing rather more openly than they would have wished. The thing was a menace. It was worse than a time bomb. Like botulism it would spread and slaughter. What to do? I rang David Attenborough only to discover he hadn't yet received his copy. Because Samantha and I worked in one of the BBC's outlying buildings it became clear that I was the first to receive a copy of the memo. Even the Director-General, to whom it was addressed, wouldn't get it until the next day. I rushed over to David's office and showed him the memo. He talked to the BBC's internal post room and discovered that by this time — it was eight in the evening — the memo would be lying in various postal in-trays. With a set of security keys we did the rounds together. In office after office, we looked for and grabbed the envelope containing the memo. Fortunately it wasn't hard to trace. They were all hand addressed in purple ink. Finally it was over.

'For God's sake, send her on holiday, keep her out of the way, promote her, sell her to ITV, but please, Desmond, never let it happen again,' said David. 'Now, am I free to go to my dinner?' It was 10 p.m.

What a splendid man, I thought, what a fine, understanding boss. I went home content. We had both forgotten one name on the list – the Head of Personnel, the formal, dignified, rose-growing gentleman himself.

The next morning, he wouldn't even explain his agitation on the telephone. He wanted me, in person. I went to his office. He looked like a turkey in its last throes. His rage was incandescent, awesome.

'That woman must be dismissed. Out. Out. Out.'

I was still very fond of Samantha and, anyway, I've always liked eccentrics. Besides, when she wasn't mad she was a very hard-working producer, and she had given a lifetime of service to the BBC, which is probably why she had gone off her rocker. Women who marry organizations instead of men eventually find the prospect of the emotional sterility ahead of them almost too much too bear – and who can blame them? Men aren't forced to make the same choice – and go barmy for other reasons.

I argued and pleaded with the Head of Personnel. I

would find a temporary job for her – in Bristol, or Leeds, or Cardiff. But it was clear that even Reykjavik would still not be far enough away. I'd send her on sick leave, I said, I'd ask her to see a specialist (the organizational euphemism for psychiatrist). But only an execution would serve the Head of Personnel. In the end I suggested the one punishment that I knew he would regard as most severe. In the whole catalogue of extermination and punishment methods used by the BBC's Personnel system, there is nothing – they think – so awful as 'the recorded interview'. It is a rocketing, delivered in person in front of a Personnel officer, written down later, read back to the miscreant, signed by the victim and the boss – and placed for ever on the individual's file. For the BBC it is the same as an order 'to dispose with extreme prejudice' given by the CIA. And that's their euphemism for assassination. I thought it was all rubbish and I knew Samantha would think it was rubbish. But the Head of Personnel pronounced himself satisfied and solemnly declared the matter closed.

Two years later he had the last laugh. I had always suspected that he actually knew I didn't have the same reverence for 'the recorded interview' that he and his men had. But he let me get away with it. He probably felt that fate, or nemesis, would be on his side, in the end. He was right.

Samantha's next explosion covered me in debris. I had, by then, married her friend Esther and we might have supposed that this would have drawn us all closer together in friendship. Not so. Samantha had fallen in love too – and her target was a young man, many years her junior, who worked closely with me.

He did not return her passion. Indeed, he was most discreet about his own private life and had never shown any sign of returning the invitations of any of the ladies in the department, who had set their caps at this respectable, good-looking bachelor. But Samantha, for some reason, decided that the young man was spurning her because he was in love with me – and I had seduced him. The existence of my wife, and our new baby, was, as far as Samantha was concerned, just a cover-up. The first I knew of all this was when she wrote a long, long letter.

It was the first of a number of long letters. Each was sent to an important person, the Director-General, the Chairman of the Board of Governors, the members of the IBA, Esther's mother and father, Sir David McNee, the Commissioner of the Metropolitan Police, Audrey Callaghan (but for some reason not her husband, who was then Prime Minister), Margaret Thatcher and the Head of Help the Aged. It went on for weeks, letter after letter, every letter copied to all the other people on the growing list. They were graphic letters, lurid with detail, descriptive about my passion for the young man, threatening about our new daughter. They were even occasionally funny, always bitingly written. It was a total blitz, it was the equivalent of the El Alamein barrage.

We discovered to our horror that some of those eminent people believed every word of the letters they received. Indeed, when we met them subsequently it was noticeable that they found it difficult to look us straight in the eye. But the thing about paranoia is that it starts as a delusion that you are being conspired against, and in the end it comes true.

So, after a while, all the friends of nice, tweedy Samantha, as shocked as we were, even frightened for her (we were becoming a little frightened for ourselves), conspired to force her to visit the doctor. He gave her some medicine and forbade her ever to see me again. She took the medicine, resigned from the BBC in a letter which, once again, she copied to everybody, saying that 'For reasons of love and heartbreak' she couldn't stay. She spent some days driving past and loitering near the young man's flat and finally found a good job in an American television company. We were all greatly relieved that the doctor had been effective, for Samantha's sake – and for our own.

Unlike our Secret Services, there seldom seems to be a scandal in television caused by gay power, or gay plotting. Of course in television – like everywhere else – there are quite a few gays, and I've always believed that is their own business.

But one ITV company for which I once worked was commanded by bristling, salty, ex-Royal Naval officers (they spent a small fortune on equipping a six-storey London building with one of the best weather stations constructed since World War II). And one of them had a phobia – gays. In those days they hadn't come out sufficiently to win general acceptance for the word 'gay'. The ex-officer didn't care about any of that. He had his own word for them, several, in fact.

After witnessing a planning meeting I had just held with one of the station's top designers, he once bellowed at me, 'That man's a damned queer, a bloody homo.' He boomed on, in tones of startled discovery. 'Get rid of him at once, do you hear? I won't have them.'

I pointed out that, if he pursued his prejudice logically, he would be responsible for dismissing a large number of the company's most talented, hard working and amusing programme people. We might fail to get on the air with some programmes and anyway, homosexuality was not, in my experience, known to be a barrier to employment – or even preferment – in television.

The good officer thought about it. 'All right, I suppose I must put up with that kind of thing in production and design – but I won't have it among the engineers. Damn it, never in the engine room.'

In British television there are whole departments that tend to be 'gay'. Certainly there are areas of design where a high degree of creativity is called for, that would be deserts of mediocrity were it not for gay talent. In some countries it also works the same way but not necessarily with the same departments. We know one Commonwealth country where all the scene shifters – a heavy, muscular, tough and dirty job – are gay. Over there leather rules, OK?

There are, of course, a number of gay reporters – most of them still in the closet and most very good at their work.

Esther once worked on a programme in the BBC when

a story came up of a man who could train earwigs to jump over fences. All the other reporters found immediate important items to work on, like the decline of the kopek or the energy crisis, or a new way to predict the sex of your baby. At the time she was sharing a desk with an extremely pleasant gay colleague and they were the only two reporters left in the production office who hadn't 'ducked' this vivid new journalistic assignment. An embarrassed researcher descended on Esther and her colleague.

'You know this man is a bit odd,' he said. 'Turns out his name's Wendy and he wears a skirt.'

The interesting thing is that Esther's gay friend at once refused to have anything to do with the story and insisted that she must cover it instead. We still don't know exactly why but he was obviously embarrassed. Incidentally, the programme never explained why Wendy the earwig trainer in a skirt and silk blouse had a deep baritone voice. The earwigs took it in their stride – and so did the viewers.

Once Esther herself was confused. She was sent, with a film crew, to interview someone who was campaigning on behalf of old age pensioners. She admits she was a little taken aback when she first met Dudley because although he was wearing trousers and Bohemian sandals he also seemed to be wearing ladies' tights. She thought 'poor old Dudley, obviously his pension doesn't run to socks'. They sat in Dudley's sitting room filming an interview about the difficulties of living on a fixed income. Suddenly Dudley pointed to a picture of a cheerful middle-aged woman on the mantelpiece and said: 'Do you recognize her?' Esther said 'No.' And he said 'That's me.' Then she realized that his slightly hippy-length grey hair only needed a little backcombing and, with a crocheted jumper instead of his hacking jacket, it was indeed him.

He explained to her that he spent most of his life as Edwina, not Dudley. He had a very understanding landlady and the biggest problem for him, living on his pension, was having to buy two wardrobes. Esther discovered for the first time how difficult it is to interview someone and at the same time try and stop him talking about the one subject he really wants to discuss. But it brought home to both of us how genuine was the agony in Dudley's life because he felt trapped in the wrong gender.

Needless to say the early evening viewers were shown a sincere interview about the problems of old age pensioners. They might have taken a little more notice if Dudley/Edwina had talked about his true problem.

9 Rows

'I don't give a sod. He's a musical performance, bleeding four-legged or not, and he needs a flaming sound assistant even if he is only four inches off the ground.' The BBC union official had spoken and Othello, the singing Dachshund, had become the centre of a controversy.

All rows are stupid, usually unnecessary and invariably unproductive. And yet sometimes all television seems to consist of is rows. I often wonder how programmes ever get made. The rows about who does what, the demarcation disputes, the staffing and feather-bedding arguments, the battles about overtime, the interminable negotiations about allowances and conditions occupy so much time in television that I have the distinct feeling that soon even the most humble film or studio director will need a union negotiator alongside him before he can use those time-honoured words 'cut', 'action' or 'quiet please, studio'. At the moment that's still a joke – but only just.

Othello was a lovely long-haired Dachshund whose young owners had taught him to count. He would bark the answer to any sum you gave him and it was impossible to see how the teenage girls of the family who trained him were cueing him. He was a natural for 'That's Life!'. A film crew was despatched immediately. Paul Heiney ran through his stock of questions for the owners of performing animals, revising some of them from the last occasion when he had interviewed the owner of a budgerigar who liked to swim with a goldfish.

When they arrived, Othello did his sums and barked the answers impeccably. The fourteen-year-old girl who had telephoned the programme told Paul: 'You know Othello also plays the piano. Well, actually he doesn't really play, he just walks up and down the keyboard wagging his tail and giving little barks. But he thinks it's playing and he always gets a biscuit for it and it might, perhaps, make a nice ending for your film, don't you think?'

She was right. The 'That's Life!' lady film director leapt at the chance. 'We'll set up here,' she told the crew. 'And then we can get a shot of Othello jumping on to the piano stool and then on to the keyboard and then we can pull back into a wide shot and it will make a lovely ending to the film.'

'Oh, no, you don't,' said the voice of doom in the shape of the lighting man. 'Not without an extra sound assistant. That's a musical performance.' And he went on to expound the nature and quality of what, in the agreement between the unions and management, constituted a 'musical performance'.

It seemed the union was having a battle with management about whether sound recordists should be allowed to travel with assistants, to help them with their equipment, like their better paid colleagues in the ITV companies. To reinforce the demand, union rules about all kinds of recording situations were being applied to the letter. But BBC sound recordists themselves are a marvellous, intelligent group of men not given to silly union postures and illogical demands. So it was always left to the most union-minded man on any film team to call for the 'work-to-rule' to be enforced.

The row that developed over Othello lasted for days and spread to the highest levels of the BBC. I could hardly believe it.

Grey-suited men, highly paid and carefully trained, debated for hours whether or not we could shoot a few seconds of film which showed Othello walking up and down the keyboard. The issue of Othello, 'a musical performance', had escalated. Should we go back and re-film Othello using an assistant sound recordist this time? Would it be a surrender on the part of the management? If we shot it without an assistant sound recordist how many more departments of the BBC would then come out on strike in sympathy?

It had finally happened. A four-year-old Dachshund had reached the highest level of union–management confrontation - it had become a matter of 'blacking'. Nobody seemed to notice that they were blacking a dog called Othello . . .

While the whole of the television service threatened to rock to a standstill Esther suggested to me that we needn't use that bit of film at all. Othello could be shown doing his sums on film and then we could cut to the studio, in front of the audience, where we would have Othello real and live – and a grand piano waiting. There would be no dispute in the studio, which is a place always full – or so it seems – of talented and willing assistant sound recordists. And so it happened. The sisters who owned Othello, stiff with pride in their party frocks, stood in the studio alongside a grand piano used only the night before by Oscar Peterson. Othello waited, quivering, for his cue. The film ended and Esther invited the girls to show what else Othello could do. One of them sat down and played 'How much is that doggy in the window?' and Othello barked the chorus. The audience went mad with applause. It may not have been Liberace but it was a musical performance. His young owners picked him up, his tail wagging with pride. Othello was no longer 'Black'.

Another row which involved animals found itself going to arbitration in the highest circles, royal circles. Esther and her team had been researching a consumer story for 'That's Life!' about a cowboy firm who fitted ramshackle central heating systems. They had discovered an unfortunate customer whose radiator, newly fitted, had developed a leak, spraying thick black oil all over his wallpaper. The customer only managed to stop the deluge by putting on the little dutch boy act and holding his thumb over the leak.

With the other hand he managed to telephone the 'con' man in charge of the central heating firm. He made his feelings plain, and after some minutes of yelling and shouting, demanded workmen to come round and repair the leak immediately – and his money back. There was a silence while the con man absorbed the fact that the anguished customer, however angry and however big, was at that moment unable to come round and thump him in person. He had to stay where his thumb was. The con man decided he could get away with the verbal equivalent of a V sign. 'You know,' he said conversationally over the telephone, 'ducks fart in church.' And he hung up.

For Esther and the team the story presented a problem. Over the years, the BBC's attitude to words and language has been a shifting territory. 'Fart' has sometimes been an acceptable word for broadcasting, sometimes not. More than that, it was an unusual phrase which she hadn't heard before. Was it the equivalent of 'Pigs might fly'? Or was it some rich piece of local dialect?

Later that night Esther and I went to a publisher's party in New Zealand House. The authors wore carnations and ordinary guests, like us, clutched our champagne gratefully. We met Sir Peter Scott, one of the authors, and Esther was unable to restrain herself.

'I have an ornithological problem for you,' she told him. 'Do ducks fart? And would they do it in church?' She explained why she needed to know. Peter Scott treated the whole matter very seriously and clearly loved the challenge.

'I haven't a clue,' he said, 'but I think I know who can help you,' and he towed us across the room to meet the Duke of Edinburgh.

'Excuse me, Sir,' he interrupted. 'But Miss Rantzen here has got a problem you may be able to help us with. She wants to know if ducks fart?' There was a moment of deep stillness in the group around His Royal Highness. Esther and I stood ready to run. Only Peter Scott, a great friend of the Duke of Edinburgh, appeared calm.

Then the Duke smiled broadly. 'You know,' he said, 'I

think they do. I'm sure they do it under water because I've always reckoned that's what those bubbles are about when they dive beneath the surface.'

If we thought union rows had gone away we were wrong. The very next week there was a big row in the BBC studios about who should operate the 'Playschool' clock, seen regularly in this highly successful children's programme, turning round and round with a model beneath it. Was it the job of a scene assistant, who'd done it before? Or a props man who'd brought the clock into the studio in the first place? Or an electrician? Regularly the Head of Children's Television, Edward Barnes, would deliver progress reports to other heads of departments at Programme Review Board. It went on for weeks. The children of the nation were clockless. Thousands of them complained. Esther and I liked to think that Emily, not quite three, was desolate. But I'm not sure she noticed.

Eventually Mr Barnes reported to a waiting television service. The dispute had been settled. None of the squabbling factions would turn the clock round. It would be switched on from the control room with a 'remote' device. Nobody at that meeting had the nerve to ask exactly how this would work, and to this day I still don't know. But I like to think they gave a signal to 'non-union' elves to run round and round inside the cogs. That's what I told Emily.

Harold Wilson was the centre of one remarkable row with the BBC. During the March 1966 election night the results made it obvious that the Conservatives weren't going to win and that Harold Wilson would still be Prime Minister of Great Britain, returned with an even greater majority. In preparation for that event ITV and the BBC had agreed to share the cost of a special train to carry Harold Wilson to London from his constituency. The train was packed with electronic equipment, turning it into a mobile studio, so that both sides could broadcast an early morning interview with Harold Wilson 'live' from a moving train – a television first.

I had joined the BBC only a few weeks before, after more

than five years on ITV's leading current affairs programme 'This Week'. Paul Fox, in charge of the BBC's election coverage, had thought it witty to offer me the 'all-through-the-night-with-the-drunks-and-the-weather' job I'd always had on election nights with ITV – in Trafalgar Square. Alan Whicker had just left the BBC for ITV – and he too had been given his usual stint in Trafalgar Square. The irony appealed to both of us. We worked, as always on election night, side by side – but, still, on opposite sides.

In the meantime the Labour landslide was building and Harold Wilson's train was due to reach Euston at breakfast time. On it, John Morgan, for the BBC, prepared to interview Harold. It's certainly true that Harold Wilson was already irritable with the BBC and had, during the election campaign, complained a number of times about their coverage. But John Morgan, as he tells it, remembers Harold Wilson passing some remark just as they were settling down to the effect, 'I hope you won't forget your loyalty to your membership of the Labour Party.' John Morgan replied, properly, but perhaps a little defensively, 'I shall remember my duty as a journalist.' Quite who said what to whom after that has been fudged in the re-telling. But there was a row, a considerable one, and Harold Wilson stormed out of the BBC's mini-studio on the train and, rather petulantly some people thought, gave an expansive interview to ITN – and nothing to the BBC.

News of the row was radioed ahead of the train direct to the BBC election control centre. It meant that ITV had scooped them with an interview with Harold Wilson. I was waiting at Euston at the time, hoping for the all-clear to go home. I'd finished my other weary election duties, vox-popping interviews with early morning commuters on what they thought of the new Labour Government. Suddenly the stage manager (the vital technical liaison in any outside broadcast unit) rushed up to me, took off his headphones and put them on my head.

Paul Fox spoke in my ears.

'Listen carefully, Desmond and give no sign to the outside

world of what I'm about to say. Just answer "yes" or "no" in your microphone.'

It was becoming more like James Bond by the minute.

'You've only been with the BBC a few weeks and Harold Wilson knows you very well from all the times you interviewed him for "This Week" and ITV. He may not even know that you've crossed over. Any minute now his train is going to come into Euston. John Morgan is on the train with a whole outside broadcast crew and there's been a flaming great row between him and Harold, the whole thing has gone up the spout because Harold has stamped out on him. So get on to the platform, stand as far away from any BBC equipment as you can, take your BBC pass out of your lapel, if you're wearing one, and see if you can grab an interview with Harold as he gets off the train.

'And if you can make him stand still for five minutes and answer one or two serious questions about the future as well as the ordinary stuff about when he expects to go to the Palace, then you'll save the day for us. I've told John Morgan not to greet you or recognize you as he gets off the train, and give the game away. Now, if you have any questions, be careful how you word them.'

At that moment a cheer went up from the crowd waiting on the platform for Harold's train. 'No questions. The train's coming in now,' I yelled into the mike. I could see the BBC cameras taking up positions where they could get a shot of the new Prime Minister coming off the train. I sprinted for the platform, tearing off my BBC pass. Two minutes later I was interviewing a victorious and affable Harold who, clearly, believed I was still a reporter on ITV's 'This Week' – at least he didn't point an accusing finger at me and say 'I accuse you of being from the BBC, get out of my sight.'

Harold Wilson stood still for nearly seven minutes and talked to me. The BBC had managed to even the balance. Paul Fox had demonstrated, once again, the tactical skill he was always able to display in tight political situations – and John Morgan and I bought each other a couple of drinks. A new era was beginning in television, a Labour Government was now firmly in office, already suspicious, even paranoid, about the BBC. It was to be the beginning of some rough years, much in-fighting and many behind-the-scenes rows. Years later I was able to tell Harold of the deception we had played on him the morning of his election. 'Oh, I wasn't deceived at all. I guessed what you were up to, and I saw no harm in giving you an interview,' he told me. I didn't believe him – and I told him so.

He gazed at me with those eyes which always look as if they are about to twinkle but seldom do. 'Ah, you don't think that I'd be daft enough ever to confirm that you and Paul Fox had put one over on me, now do you?' he said.

The night a row took Miss World off the air was a night that Esther and I won't forget easily. Esther had been asked to interview the finalists. She had, some months earlier, inter- viewed the girls in the Miss United Kingdom contest and the critics had been kind enough to praise her efforts because the girls had been allowed more time to answer more sensible questions. Naturally the BBC producer wanted Esther to repeat her success for the Miss World Competition. But Esther was eight months pregnant, seated on a stool in a series of chiffon layers designed by the marvellous Head of BBC Costumes, Peter Shepherd, who had spent the whole time muttering, 'I'm nothing but a camouflage expert. Next week it'll be circular tents.'

For two exhausting days the whole complicated show had been rehearsed in the Royal Albert Hall. Struggling with the acoustics of that impossible building, coping with the Babel of many languages and quite a few cases of hysterics, the highly skilled outside broadcast team had laboured to produce – as they always did – a polished and skilful broad- cast.

Within the BBC, a union row had been boiling for days over the 'grading' and payment scales of various technical staff levels. As part of the union fight they had already 'struck' a number of vulnerable productions.

They struck Miss World. At first the sound men and camera men who had worked so hard to produce a programme they could be proud of, refused to walk out on an occasion which would take place in a few hours' time in front of three thousand people in the Albert Hall, and would be broadcast to three hundred million people around the world. A union official was despatched to the Albert Hall to deal with the crews. They gave him a hard time. But in the end he won and the men walked out on the production. There was no broadcast. Several of the crew, proud of their work, were in tears and one or two deliberately tore up their union cards. Union rows always hurt.

But it was a row about the fuzzy wigs we bought in Shepherd's Bush street market for a tribe of missionary-eating cannibals in West Africa that became almost gothic in its style. Actually, the Fan tribe in Sierra Leone no longer eat missionaries, or even each other, but they used to, and they had very willingly agreed to co-operate with one of my department's production teams which was filming drama documentaries on the lives of great explorers. Executive producer Michael Latham and the director, Lord Snowdon, wanted the journeys of a famous Victorian lady explorer, Mary Kingsley, filmed where she actually made them. So off they went for a reconnaissance with the designer and the cameramen. They found the Fan natives, the tribe that had decided not to eat Mary Kingsley, living much as they had in her days. Their huts were made by weaving local trees and creepers. The situation was ideal for their film. Tony Snowdon was delighted, the cameraman got excited – the designer was cautious. All the illustrations he'd seen in his careful research of Mary Kingsley's explorations showed the Fan natives with much 'fuzzier' hair than their descendants.

'We'll have to have fuzzy-wuzzy wigs,' he announced firmly. 'Afro wigs, then they'll begin to look like real West African natives.'

'But they are real West African natives. Damn it, they're the *real* natives of the real tribe. They *are* the Fan,' said Tony

Snowdon. But the designer prevailed and compromised only to the extent of agreeing to buy cheap fuzzy-wuzzy wigs, £2.50 each.

The wigs, fifty of them, were purchased, packed and despatched to Sierra Leone. One or two of the Fan natives reluctantly agreed to wear the nylon disco-wigs from Shepherd's Bush. When shooting was over, the wigs were returned to London to become part of the BBC's stock. They were forgotten by the crew in West Africa, who were already deep in another row caused by a union official insisting that a studio carpenter should travel to West Africa and stand by while the Fan natives plaited and weaved several huts especially for the filming, a job they'd been doing for generations, a job the carpenter could not in any case have done. That row was complicated further by the insistence of the union man that a painter should also go on location in case the huts needed painting.

Months later Lord Snowdon was preparing to shoot yet another episode in the 'Explorers' series, this time in Australia, on the extraordinary journey of Burke and Wills who crossed the interior deserts and died tragically. The drama documentary had several scenes with aborigines in them and Tony Snowdon agreed that this time the fuzzy-wuzzy wigs might be useful to restore the aborigines to the hairstyles they had worn a hundred years earlier. The Shepherd's Bush disco/afro specials came painfully back into his memory. The designer agreed to dig them out and use them on location.

Subsequently I had to soothe both Lord Snowdon and Michael Latham when they arrived in my office virtually incoherent with rage. They had discovered that their budget was over-spent. Producers are kept strictly to budget, to over-spend is a crime and means trouble in the future – costing programmes or promotion. The reason for their 'crime' was not their fault but was because the BBC make-up department had charged for the hire of the wigs at £2.50 per wig, per day, for nearly six weeks. A bill of £5,550 for a bunch of nylon 'tat' we ourselves had purchased in the first place, from a market stall for about £150 the lot.

In the ensueing correspondence between heads of service departments tempers were lost and polite language obscured. At one time, raging with fury at an obscure and convoluted reply, explaining why something my department had bought in the first place and then given to the make-up department could be rented back to us so exorbitantly, I committed an error. I wrote to my colleague, 'Don't you swing your handbag at me, Ducky-Boots'. It was incautious of me and not forgotten by him. I never succeeded in patching up that quarrel.

On the same drama documentary series we nearly caused the newly promoted Managing Director of BBC Television, Alasdair Milne, to have a heart attack. He was on his way to New York on BBC business when he recognized a studio props-man sauntering through the Air Terminal at Kennedy Airport. He said 'Hello' and asked what business had brought him to Manhattan.

'Oh, I'm not staying in New York, I'm going on to Rio and then all the way down to somewhere near Tierra del Fuego. They're filming the Captain Cook episode in 'Explorers' down there and I've got to take them a suitcase full of "non-burning snow".'

Non-burning snow is, in fact, a chemical powder which looks like snow and can be used in scenes where the actors may have to touch it. The normal powders cause itching skin and red sores, but Alasdair Milne couldn't have been expected to know details like that. All he could see was one man and a suitcase flying down to Rio and he couldn't work out why the suitcase couldn't go on its own. He was incensed by sending the man – and the thousands of pounds in fares. He was quite explosive about it on the phone to me – particularly considering he had taken the trouble to find a phone in the airport and get through to London in order to express his opinion. Later I discovered that the unions had insisted on the snow having a personal chaperone. But that was too late to stop my boss bending my ear.

In the end I agreed with him, in my opinion the scene with the precious non-burning snow, which was played out on the poop deck on Captain Cook's *Endeavour*, wasn't worth it. They could just as well have done without. A discovery, like many, I made too late.

But the rows that remain most affectionately in our memory are usually those to do with censorship. The internal censorship based on rules which rely on 'taste' decided by the bosses. For example, for years they decided that bare breasts were not allowed to be shown on the television screen in this country – unless they were brown. So in programmes like 'The World About Us', for which I was responsible, you could, long before the children's bedtime, see attractive topless brown ladies – but not white. It was probably becoming accustomed to this form of 'double-think' that led me into trouble with Time-Life films, the BBC's syndication agents and co-producers of the Explorers series. In the same Captain Cook episode that featured the non-burning snow there was a charming and idyllic scene of the crew of the *Endeavour*, in Tahiti, swimming with naked maidens, which created a mighty row in America.

Over there at least they didn't have a double standard. Black, white, yellow, brown or striped – if they weren't covered up, you couldn't show them. The scene was cut out.

Mary Whitehouse has, of course, created many a row. Both of us are very fond of this fierce campaigner, and have debated with her on and off television many times. But she is guilty in our opinion of a slightly sharp debating trick. Once, appearing with Esther at a Bristol University Union debate, she was arguing passionately for more control in television and in society as a whole.

In the course of her speech she said that the increased sale of pornography on open display in Denmark had led to an increase in sex crimes, particularly against children. It was a telling point, difficult to argue against. The problem was, it wasn't altogether true. But you can't, in the middle of a debate, check statistics, figures or facts brought forward by the other side. The unspoken rules of such occasions place responsibility on both sides to make sure they get their figures right and their homework accurate.

Mary has since remained unrepentant. She believes there are several ways to translate figures and that the only way to use them is to win the argument. Esther and I don't agree with her, but good luck to her.

The things that Mary Whitehouse gets cross about have always, in fact, been the subjects of much internal censorship in both ITV and the BBC. In the 1950s, the BBC even produced a rule book. In it they listed not only the words you could not use on the air, but also the jokes and the references you should never broadcast. You were not allowed in the BBC to use the old jokes about what makes a Maltese Cross or Brass Monkey weather. At one time there was a huge list of 'Thou shalt nots'. You were not supposed to swear, make fun of religion, royalty, sex, another person's sexual deviation or physical disability. When Frank Muir, who was the BBC's Head of Comedy for many years, left the Corporation to continue with his highly successful comedy writing career in ITV, he swore that the first sentence he would insert into the first comedy he produced would have a character say: '"Good Lord," said the Queen, "I think that one-legged Chinaman over there is a bloody poofter ..."'

Those rules still largely apply and so we find it surprising that very popular comedians like Bernard Manning trade successfully on jokes about racial prejudice. But then our prejudice is disliking jokes about racial prejudice.

10 'A Television Personality'

Concorde flight number BA 188 from Washington, was making its final approach to London. The passengers tightened their seat belts and prepared for landing. I waited, with Lizzie our young nanny and Emily, aged six weeks, for Esther to come out from the flight deck. She'd been there a long time and although that hadn't made me nervous I could see from the glances of the other passengers that they thought that 'telly personality' or not, the flight deck of the world's first supersonic airliner was no place for Esther Rantzen to be, while it was landing. Still she didn't appear. Several passengers retightened their seat belts.

I began to get irritable. 'Flashy show-off,' I thought. We were returning from a trip to Florida where I had been sent to promote the BBC television series 'Americans' and a Florida banking firm who had bought the series had pleasantly insisted that my wife and brand new baby should come too. So, they'd both had a nice time by the poolside in Key Biscayne, with lots of elderly Manhattan grandmothers cooing over the new born Emily – 'Have a nice day, enjoy your baby' – while I was jetted round the state twelve hours a day appearing on dozens of local chat shows to explain why an Englishman, and a British broadcasting organization, had the temerity to produce a series of documentaries on Americans. Now we were returning.

This was Esther's first flight on Concorde and she was as impressed as everybody always is by this 'Star Trek' experience. So when the Captain sent a message back inviting her to come and have a look at 'the office' she shot up the centre aisle of the plane at supersonic speed. 'Oh yes,' I murmured to her departing back. 'Life in the goldfish bowl can really be hell . . .'

All the same, it was all wrong – I thought – that she should still be there during landing. My thoughts on the subject were interrupted by the landing itself. I am not a veteran of Concorde landings but the man across the aisle from me was and we both agreed that the plane should not have bounced as high, or as often, as it did. There were angry looks from some of the passengers, particularly when, as we taxied to the terminal, a sheepish-looking Esther emerged from the flight deck.

'Oh, my God,' said the man across the aisle. 'The silly bugger let her land it.' He appeared to be about to have his first coronary. Esther slid into her seat alongside me.

'What the hell were you doing up there?' I muttered.

'Tell you later,' she said.

Afterwards she explained that she had been sitting quietly in the back of the flight deck as the Captain explained they were, on that trip, also training another pilot and all pilots enjoy landing a plane like Concorde manually even though its advanced instrumentation would allow a perfectly smooth automatic landing. Suddenly, when they had only been fifty feet or so above the end of the runway, red lights started flashing on and off all over the cockpit and alarm buzzers sounded insistently. The engineer leaned past Esther yelling 'Take out the automatic,' or some such technical phrase. Immediately the Captain and his co-pilot had flicked a switch. The red lights had gone out, the alarm buzzers stopped. It appeared that they had left the controls locked on automatic but were still trying to land the plane manually. By the time they'd switched fully over to manual it was too late to avoid a bump, several bumps in fact. The high-bridged nose nearly got a nasty bruise – quite a dangerous one. The problem had clearly been caused by some kind of flying 'machismo' because the highly skilled pilots very much wanted to 'fly' the machine rather than let the automatic instruments handle it. After they'd landed, Esther told me, there was a strange silence on the flight deck. The atmosphere was oppressive with people not speaking. It was obvious they all wanted to have a row, somebody needed to shout. She left.

To be invited by the Captain of Concorde to watch the dazzling display of dials is very flattering – a perk of the 'television personality' business. Actually, anybody can be a telly personality. It only takes a few appearances on the screen and, such is the power of the box in the corner, recognition is instant. The penalty is that you are peered at like a goldfish in a bowl. People are usually very polite – if they loathe you and your work they usually don't tell you to your face. Of course, private life can become almost impossible to achieve and the penalty of being recognized can sometimes seem unbearable. But we all know the rules: if you can't stand the heat get out of the kitchen. And it would be untrue, and ungracious, to pretend that it is anything other than highly flattering and very pleasing when people are nice to you because of the telly.

Although it *is* nice to be recognized in public, in shops, Esther tends to find all the salesmen cowering behind the staff door drawing lots among themselves as to who should serve her, for fear that she is on a consumer investigation. It also means that you can't have arguments in public, or behave as rudely as you might want to towards other drivers. In any case, it is vital to remember that it's just as easy to stop being a telly personality as it is to become one.

For us, the real telly personalities are the marvellous and talented performers like Mike Yarwood, Janet Brown and many others that we've been privileged to meet just because we've managed to join the minor ranks of the same league. I found it fascinating to discover that Mike Yarwood finds it difficult actually to be himself. Any conversation with him is invariably punctuated with the voices of the characters in his repertoire. If he wants to be rude, or just forthright, you'll suddenly find yourself listening to Harold Wilson or Len Murray. Clearly a very shy man himself, he uses the voices of less shy people to express himself, and tick people off. It sometimes makes it almost impossible to discover the real personality behind the creative impersonation. But, in all our lives, there must have been many occasions when it would have been a huge relief to be able to switch to somebody else's character in order to deliver a few home truths, to a boss or a critic.

Janet Brown on the other hand uses a different approach to get close to her 'victims'. We have been friends with her for some time and have now become quite used, when she pops round for tea or supper, to see her heading straight for the bedroom and Esther's wardrobe in order to check on what kind of clothes Esther wears. She then goes to the same shop, to buy identical models. When I persuaded Esther to cut her hair short Janet Brown was devastated and more than a little cross with me. Thames Television, it seems, had just invested in a number of Rantzen wigs for Janet to wear – all at the old length and now all at the wrong length.

Huw Wheldon spent most of his television career behind the camera – perhaps the most creative influence on television of our time – but at the same time remained a sought-after personality. He would have become a personality, in my opinion, even without television. He has one of the most positively commanding manners you could ever witness in public. His speeches are witty, literate, filled with jokes and charm, always to the point and invariably effective. But they are not short. Once he became a senior executive in the BBC he saw no reason why he should have to curtail or cut down material which he – and, to be fair, the rest of us – thought effective at length. He developed, therefore, an opening habit which I've often wished I had the nerve to emulate. He would stand up, look at his wristwatch, sometimes take it off and put it on the table in front of him, and say to whatever group he was addressing:

'I propose to speak, now, for fifty-two or fifty-three minutes – it may be as long as fifty-six minutes and I shall then allow a little time for sensible questions.'

David Attenborough is not only another executive who has become a television personality himself but so have many of the animals and creatures he has brought to the screen. Shortly after I'd joined the BBC to work for David on BBC-2 he told me that he had named one of his pet bushbabies Desmond. With their huge liquid eyes and furry faces I've always thought them charming. I was flattered and asked why.

'Well I like to call my pets after telly personalities,' he said with a grin. 'And anyway, it seems appropriate.'

'Why appropriate?'

'You see, this bushbaby has a habit that somehow reminds me of your more impulsive moments. He's taken to peeing on his hands and then making palm prints all over the wall ...'

I was never quite so fond of bushbabies after that.

The viewers might re-evaluate some of the personalities they see regularly on their screens if they knew what went on behind the screen – or just before that moment when they appear. Everybody gets nerves – it takes people differently. Ludovic Kennedy compulsively eats the small piles of square-cut BBC sandwiches provided in the pre-programme hospitality rooms. If it's ever seemed, as the camera has cut to him, that he's just been swallowing a mouthful of food, then he has. Esther, when she gave up smoking, took to chewing gum – a habit that sent me into frenzies of personal irritation – but as yet she's always remembered to get rid of it before appearing on the air.

For the first few years that I appeared live each week on 'This Week', my stomach would become so tense that I would usually throw up afterwards. Not immediately afterwards but, unfortunately and expensively, usually only a couple of hours after I'd been out to a restaurant and had a good dinner

There are very few people I know who would try and pretend that there isn't at least some tightening of the nerves, a tensing of the stomach muscles, at the moment the red light comes on. Indeed, most good television performances depend on precisely that kind of adrenalin. The director and the producer will feel it just as much. And the real moment of truth for the front person is when machines fail. It means the control room has to be able to talk to the presenter, to explain. It means, therefore, earpieces – not for the deaf but the needy. Nowadays, while a programme is running, the control room will keep technical information flowing to the presenter through an earpiece.

Most viewers have, by now, stopped believing that Peter Woods, Hugh Scully, Bob Wellings and others, are unfortunately deaf and wearing hearing aids. Women find they can conceal these communication earpieces more easily under their hair.

In complicated and difficult 'live' sporting programmes like 'Grandstand', in which Frank Bough has demonstrated such mastery, they also feed into his earpiece the countdowns as they roll film and video tape inserts and many other programme instructions. How he manages to sound intelligible, and not go cross-eyed while listening to all those voices counting backwards from ten, calling instructions to cameras and sound men, is a source of wonderment and admiration among all the professionals. He once confessed to me that he's become so used to wearing his earpiece that at the end of one five-hour stint on the air with 'Grandstand' he drove home with it still in position, the length of hollow plastic tube hanging down his back.

I was wearing one once, at the insistence of a rather nervous producer who suggested that, while I was chairing a 'Man Alive' debate, he would need to encourage me, and issue further instructions. During those complicated large debates I usually didn't wear earpieces – I felt there was always enough going on in front of the cameras without added complications.

But Ivor Dunkerton is a talented and persuasive producer, basically a film maker and not so familiar with studio operation. Now, the trick about giving instructions into earpieces is to make what you have to say brief, to speak only when the person wearing the earpiece isn't also speaking – it will send him mad otherwise – and never to pose a question to the man in front of camera. After all, he can't talk back without revealing everything to the viewers.

We were half-way through the debate when Ivor's voice sounded in my ear. The earpiece voice always drowns out the 'real' sound round you. Conversationally, amiably, he said:

'Desmond, we've been having a little talk up here in the control room and we're a bit bothered about the issues dealt with in the first section. We think that some of the people in the argument didn't really speak as fully as they could. On the other hand you may feel that what's happening now is rather more interesting and you might not want to interrupt it in order to come back to that earlier point.'

By now I was almost squinting as Ivor went on:

'It's also a bit of a problem because there are only seven or eight minutes left of the programme and I know you want to come to the MPs by the end of the debate. Now, what do you think we should do . . . ?'

Thank God for large 'Man Alive' debates. Fortunately most of the participants had continued vigorously to argue with each other and failed to notice the kind of rigor which had descended on their chairman. That had been no brief instruction in my ear. That had been a long and interesting speech and an extremely complicated question. It was, of course, impossible to reply. I tell myself I am not bad tempered or indulgent when it comes to professional behaviour. Nevertheless, I do not regret what I did that night. Slowly and calmly, so that it could be seen on the monitor screens in the control room, I took out my earpiece. I put it on the floor. And I stamped on it. The debate continued with vigour and Ivor Dunkerton forgave my rude gesture – and I forgave his enthusiastic mistake.

*

Being a telly personality also means being asked for autographs. It's part of the price and a fair one. It is, sometimes, surprising how many famous people irritably refuse autographs – even when asked by children. Esther was once taking a young cousin of hers on a trip round the BBC Television Centre when they spotted, in the canteen, a famous film star who was appearing in a BBC play. In heroic films about wartime adventures he was invariably the calm, affectionate Englishman. He'd starred in dramas and comedies and had a reputation for charm and generosity. The little girl went up to him and said timidly:

'Would you mind if I asked for your autograph please?'

He said, 'Oh God, I thought we could get away from all that in here.'

The young girl blushed to the roots of her hair and retreated in confusion. To this day Esther cannot watch that distinguished actor's movies without growling. He may not have realized the damage he'd done, but he's not the only one.

Taking a child in care from the Camden home where Esther was an official 'Aunt' round the studios once, Esther met Sheila Hancock accompanied by a famous lady academic who had become a telly star because of her vigorous and outspoken arguments about women's liberation and the role of women in society. Naturally, the child wanted autographs. Esther asked if they minded. The lady academic replied tartly, 'No, but I'd think it pretty wet.' The child was confused and started to back away. Sheila Hancock saved the day by saying to her, 'I'd like to give you an autograph if you want it.' It was a lesson neither of us forgot.

There is, though, an observation that we've since made ourselves. Most people when asking you for an autograph say 'it's for my mother, daughter, son, friend' – anybody but themselves. Only children ask you directly for your autograph – then they ask for twenty-five at a time. And being recognized can cut both ways. Bernard Braden once told me about an evening he spent in a smart Italian restaurant. As he sat down, all round the room people recognized him. It's a condition he's been used to during a long working life in the limelight. Suddenly, he spotted somebody he, himself, knew in the far corner of the restaurant and started to wave vigorously. But equally suddenly he stopped waving. He told me:

'Because you've seen somebody on the screen you think you know them. I'd been waving at Princess Anne.'

Esther, Emily and I went for a quiet weekend once, with our new nanny, Jayne. We chose a hotel only fifteen miles from Cambridge because Esther was addressing a meeting of the National Childbirth Trust there and because we wanted to be near Esther's sister's family. The idea was to get away from work pressure, London, television and to relax in a quiet country hotel.

It was beautifully set in the heart of racecourse country. The first evening at the hotel, while Esther was delivering her lecture, I arranged to read Emily a story and then to meet our nanny in the bar before dinner. When I got to the bar Jayne was looking round-eyed with intrigue.

'Those men with those two women in the corner,' she said, 'have been talking about you. They keep saying who is she? What's she up to? I'll bet he's at it. I think they mean that you're here on a naughty weekend. They think it's with me.' She blushed.

I glanced at the group in the corner who were clearly enjoying quite a few pre-dinner drinks, large ones, and equally clearly had dirty minds. Nanny was right. The glances and nudging told their own story. Jayne is a very pretty girl, she wasn't wearing a uniform and the gang in the corner hadn't seen a baby – or any evidence of Esther.

Throughout dinner the glancing and the nudging continued. Later, while having coffee in the lounge Esther rejoined us. 'That's one in the eye for that gang,' I thought. At that moment a large hand descended on Esther's shoulder from behind.

'I just thought we'd say hello,' said the leader of the gang.

He was the editor of the *Sun* newspaper. He, and his senior staff, had come for a weekend conference and had chosen the hotel we had retreated to as an escape. Thank heavens Esther came back from the lecture that night. If she'd stayed overnight with her sister in Cambridge there's no knowing what story might have been in the gossip columns. And the reputation of nanny Jayne would never have been the same again.

These days, part of the price of being a telly personality, willingly or unwillingly, is the fact that newspapers are avid for stories about the telly and its people. Not always the stories you would want printed. There was the time, in 1977, when Esther and I went through our first experience of being 'staked out' by the press, subsequently it's happened several times and we have even become old hands at the game. Then, it was a silly-season story about Esther and the future of 'That's Life!'. We had decided to ignore the inquiries and not to be drawn. Anyway, Esther was four months pregnant with Emily and had been warned by her doctor that the pregnancy was at a vulnerable stage, she was even likely to lose the baby, and she should stay in bed for at least ten days. We, therefore, had other things on our minds. Notwithstanding, we were besieged by the press – staked out.

A 'stake out' is a journalistic siege. At the time we lived in a beautiful house, overlooking the River Thames on one side and thousands of acres of open fields on the other. There could have been worse places to be under siege. I left Esther in bed contentedly answering letters with her secretary, Janice, while I went to work. During the course of the day I checked progress on the phone. It was a cold wintery day, raining frequently. The journalists on 'stake out' stuck to their posts. Esther told me that at one stage the reporter from the *Evening News* went away on his motorbike to collect Chinese food for everybody. But apart from that they remained persistent. When Tony Kinsey, then the musical director of 'That's Life!', called in to chat to her, he was bothered about what would happen when he left and the reporters asked him questions.

'Stick a pencil behind your ear and pretend you've just been checking the central heating,' Esther suggested.

He did and left the front door muttering 'I don't know nothing mate, I'm just part of the workforce round 'ere, don't know nothing.' Tony Kinsey is a brilliant musician but a reasonably terrible actor. However it worked. The 'stake out' parted its ranks and let him through.

Later when I came home I was irritated to find the siege still in progress, but not as irritated as the tough young woman in a grey flannel skirt from the *Daily Express* who charged at me as I put my key in the door and said:

'Do you know how cold and wet we've all been getting waiting out here? What have you got to say to that?'

As a journalist I like my fellow professionals, I understand and admire the good ones and I even understand, without admiration, the bad ones. I hope I may be forgiven my reply.

'Good,' I said.

The moral of that story, Esther insists, is if you're lying in bed, on doctor's orders, and enjoying it, don't worry about what's going on outside. It's the best way to survive a stake out.

Some years later we were staked out again, at another house. The lady reporter and her photographer colleague actually emerged from behind the rhododendron bushes as we unloaded the children from the car on our return from a birthday party. This time we were being polite but trying also to be silent. We thought. I smiled and nodded, as did Esther, at the questions and went on decanting the children. Finally, when the lady reporter shrilled, 'Would you say today that you are both the victims of an assassin's plot?' I nearly dropped the baby, murmured absentmindedly, 'Something like that,' and then accidentally trod on the photographer's spectacles which he had placed on the door-step while he focussed his camera. It needed no guesswork to foretell the quote and the headlines that appeared in the paper the next day: 'I've been victim of plot: says BBC man'.

When Esther and I got married more than a dozen photographers turned up at the Register Office and there were several at the reception. Afterwards we went home to change and drive away for a weekend, we were both due back at work on the Monday. We relaxed and had a drink, the formal proceedings behind us. There was a ring at the doorbell. We had reckoned without a couple of Fleet Street photographers who had missed both the wedding and the reception. There are always some who do. The Biblical story about the foolish virgins sprang to mind but didn't seem entirely appropriate.

There were two photographers and we gently suggested to them that we wanted to get away on our forty-eight-hour honeymoon and would like to say 'no' to more pictures. The two hard men at the door were adamant. 'You can ask us in – or you can force us to stake you out,' one said. 'If we come inside we'll be quick and take a good picture. Otherwise it'll be flash taken at night, as you come out through the door and it'll make you look like bank robbers trying to escape.' We invited them in. Their offer was one we couldn't refuse and it certainly wasn't a day when we wished to be staked out.

They posed us on the sofa, leaning heads together, holding glasses of imaginary champagne, in fact it was water. In those two papers the next morning we both looked completely smashed and silly. It would have been better to run and look like bank robbers.

Photographers always want 'that day's' picture of anybody they deem to be a television personality. Choosing between the dozens that may be available in a newspaper's picture library is too easy. The first time Esther was photographed as a 'personality' was shortly after she'd been chosen to appear with John Pitman on 'Braden's Week'. She told me afterwards:

'He was an odd man, he made me sit on the edge of a desk with my legs crossed and then he lay down on the floor with his camera and looked up at me. I can't think why.'

I could. I'd been too long in Fleet Street myself. When the picture appeared Esther had learned lesson number one – be careful how much leg you are persuaded to show.

She learned lesson number two just as hard. A famous photographer had been commissioned to take a photograph of her for a Sunday newspaper series. He invited her to his studio. She was wearing a V-neck blouse and a smart skirt. He unrolled about ten yards of ten foot wide white paper on the floor and asked her to lie down on it, on her stomach with her elbows and her hands in front of her like the paws of a sphynx.

'It makes the bones of your face look good,' he said with the kind of flattery no woman can ever resist. 'And it gives the best lighting.' Then he lay down facing Esther and took the photograph. Lesson number two is never be persuaded to show too much cleavage.

Telly personalities are, of course, always useful for making speeches, opening fetes and attending functions to help charities. But even with gratitude people will slap you in the face. Cyril Fletcher, one of the most experienced men we know at travelling round the country and speaking in public, calls it 'being insulted by professionals' and he means it kindly. He once agreed to put on his complicated and demanding one-man show in order to raise funds for the repair of a church roof. He arrived with his accompanist and some props, and found every seat had been sold. Three hours later he'd finished his show and the collection had been taken. The roof was saved.

A week later he received a letter from the vicar which said, 'Thank you for your efforts. You will be pleased to hear that, so far, there have been no complaints.'

I once lectured at a terrifying ladies' luncheon club in the north. Eight hundred women in hats, determined to be entertained – and me. There was one other man, the mayor of the local town, the husband of the forceful lady chairwoman. She explained: 'We brought him along because we looked at your picture and saw that you were middle-aged as well, and we thought you might like to go to the gents some time and it would be less embarrassing if you had a man to show you the way . . .'

We have also been privileged to find out about telly personalities - and their loos. One famous lady uses the walls of her loo to hang hundreds of proof photographs of herself. I don't care what it may reveal about her ego, I still found it fascinating and stayed in there for hours. Michael Bentine keeps a whole set of *Encyclopaedia Britannica* in his loo and for all we know he may stay in there for weeks.

And in the Television Theatre at Shepherd's Bush there is a loo, seldom glimpsed by ordinary mortals. It appears to be almost completely decorated in purple velvet. It is quite overwhelming. In our humble opinion it would be almost impossible to perform any natural function at all there.

Mind you, we've never been asked to try. It was specially decorated before the last visit of the Queen to the BBC Television Theatre. I can't discover if she went there.

One disadvantage of being a lady television personality is that you become a fantasy figure of a seamier kind. Esther was once filming with a cameraman who insisted on telling her of his nights of steamy passion on foreign locations with a highly talented international lady singing star. He went into the sort of personal detail he wouldn't dream of talking about, had it been his wife he was remembering. Was it perhaps not true? We had our doubts.

One evening, later, driving through Kensington in her mini, Esther had one of those accidents that have been known to happen to her – a traffic bollard reversed into her radiator. Annoyed with herself she got out of the car to inspect the damage. A passer-by interferingly said:

'I saw that happen, you drove into it. What's more I know you.'

Esther denied it.

'Ah, I haven't met you myself but you were in Israel on holiday recently and there was a friend of mine there, you know him, Peter – the racing driver. You got to know him very well, you know what I mean, really very well indeed. And he's a great friend of mine,' said this unpleasant stranger on a Kensington pavement. Esther had not met the racing driver. What was clear was that he had chosen to boast about a conquest he'd never made. We've since discovered that this is not an uncommon claim. Part of the price of being a lady telly personality, it seems, is to find yourself claimed as a trophy.

Another price is that you're also always expected to do a party turn. We both remember Frankie Howard being brilliantly funny during one edition of 'Braden's Week'. Afterwards, in the hospitality Green Room as everybody urged him to go on, he complained that he was really a sad and shy person and that it was almost impossible for him to 'turn on at will'. He then kept us all in stitches for another hour.

The next week the same thing happened rather more embarrassingly for us. Esther had been interviewing Eartha Kitt on a programme and afterwards Esther's mother wandered up to Eartha. 'Go on, give us a song then,' she said in a friendly attempt to break the ice. We vanished.

Occasionally an overnight television personality can be created by accident. It can even happen to a bishop. During an edition of a late night satire show the Bishop was being interviewed in a segment of the programme always referred to as 'the conversation'. The Bishop was more than conversational. He was indefatigable – and unstoppable. The producer in charge in the control room gave the instruction to the floor manager 'Wind him', the signal to conclude the interview. The interviewer had been unable even to find a breath pause into which to step and say 'Thank you' to end it. Therefore, unusually, the signal was now being given directly to the person being interviewed. The floor manager gave the standard television signal, a continuous circling motion of the forefinger. The Bishop's eyes widened slightly but his flow didn't pause. Slowly his own hand came into vision as he imitated the floor manager's circling motion The viewers must have thought he was going mad.

From the control room the producer ordered 'give him a throat-cut'. This is the slashing gesture across the throat that is a professional signal to stop as quickly as possible. The effect on the Bishop, finger still circling, was only to make him speak quicker, almost falsetto. Finally the producer commanded 'try jumping up and down in front of him'. The floor manager jumped – tongue hanging out, eyes crossed.

At last the Bishop stopped. He rose to his feet, still on camera and, in his purple cassock gaiters started to jump up and down, with his tongue stuck out. The producer gave up, and, at last, the interviewer was able to lean forward and say, 'Thank you, Bishop'.

At ecclesiastical tea parties, for years after, people would wander up to the Bishop, do a 'double take' and then say: 'Come on, Bishop, do a jump for us.' Such is the price of becoming a 'television personality'.

11 Does the camera lie?

Yes, the camera does lie. The man confronting Esther in the crowd at London Airport was really quite belligerent about it. 'Why are you so small?' he said accusingly. 'You're actually tiny. I mean, not just smaller than I thought – but really small, tiny.' There was no answer to that.

As I had just suspended all our hand baggage from her shoulders and shoved my briefcase into her hand while I searched for her passport yet again (in the end, unsurprisingly, we missed the flight because she'd left it at home), it was astonishing that she was recognizable at all under the mountain of our combined luggage.

But the 'tricks' produced by television cameras on the television screens are sometimes quite startling, even for those of us who work in the industry. Esther looks six feet tall instead of five feet three. It it difficult to gauge a person's true size or shape in real life when you only ever see them in the artificial perspective of a studio, usually with only their faces in large close up. And it does produce, for some people, an almost aggressive feeling of having been cheated when viewers discover the truth for themselves, that TV giants are often real-life pygmies.

It also leads to pleasant surprises. We often wondered how many people who watched Angela Rippon read the news, in that severely precise way, would ever find out what a slender, bubbly person she is, and how different she looks when she isn't seriously addressing the camera. Now she's out and about in other programmes it's possible that more people will learn the pleasant truth.

Of course, a great deal of television is introduced by people sitting down, often behind desks or tables; so there is an extraordinary amount of speculation about their legs – have they got any? What colour are Richard Baker's socks? And, however accurate the television camera is, it is always two dimensional – turning people into cardboard cut-outs of themselves. It never quite reproduces their true complexion or hair colour. The camera does, in fact, lie. At the same time, television is a kind of X-ray medium. It somehow sees beneath the skin. Through the lens, viewers can move much closer to the face of somebody speaking than they would in real life, gaze more carefully at the eyes of a person in argument. As certain politicians have found to their dismay, deceit and trickery are difficult to get away with. Television can be ruthless to those who lie. Falseness tends to come across to the viewers. Hustlers are seen for what they are. But just occasionally we have come across occasions when the cameras have been deliberately used to tell a lie – to the delight of viewers.

On one occasion we ourselves were completely conned by a lady who came to be interviewed on 'Junior That's Life!'

We were running a contest to find the granny with the most terrible singing voice. They were nominated by their grandchildren and they all entered cheerfully into the spirit of the competition by agreeing to be filmed in heats in church halls round the country singing at maximum volume – a noise none of us will ever forget. Each granny wore her favourite evening dress and we supplied a hairdresser and beauty treatment for them so they all thoroughly enjoyed their day.

The problem arose when Dolly White arrived to be filmed

in her local church hall. In spite of the fact that her hair looked like a bird's nest and she'd forgotten to put her teeth in, she still adamantly refused to let the make-up lady put even a dab of powder on her nose. But she was wonderfully funny and an outrageously bad singer.

When Esther saw the film in a viewing room she was entranced. Granny Dolly even improvised a little dance to round off her off-key bellowed musical performance. Esther stopped the viewing machine and said to her colleagues: 'She's marvellous – but she's having us on.' It was quite obviously a brilliant and highly professional impersonation of a granny. But the whole of the 'Junior That's Life!' team were already in love with the performance. If they challenged her they might discover something which would mean they would have to disqualify her. The decided to let sleeping dogs lie – or singing grannies tell a fib.

At the finals, in the studio, everybody's suspicions should have been confirmed. Dolly White's hair was even more of a bird's nest and once again she'd left her teeth behind. She still adamantly refused the help of the BBC make-up lady.

Nevertheless she was one of the most popular finalists. The studio audience loved her. In the end Les Dawson, the judge, decided that lovely Rene with flowing blonde hair just outpointed Granny Dolly by a short screech.

It's as well he did. A month after the event Dolly wrote to us and 'confessed'. She wasn't a granny at all, she had borrowed a 'grandson' to sponsor her. And the routine that Esther had spotted as a nearly professional comic turn was the act she used to entertain her friends in the local pub. She's actually a jolly lady in her forties – and she still sends us Christmas cards.

If you tell a lie and you're found out then of course you must say sorry, apologize. But an apology in television is usually something forced on to the screen by pressure from lawyers, past the resistance of programme makers who cannot bear the thought of publicly admitting that they were wrong. But one man did it with a style that we've never seen bettered. Michael

Bunce, now Head of BBC Television's Information Services (the press officers and publicity officers) was editor of 'The Money Programme' when they made a mistake in a story about Isaac Woolfson.

An apology was demanded and, because the programme had to confess to an error, it was conceded. Some programme editors would have gritted their teeth and then fought to ensure that the apology went out somewhere between the weather forecast and a party political broadcast, preferably close to midnight – or at nine a.m. on a Sunday morning, just before the lessons in differential calculus.

But Michael Bunce is a cool hand. He commissioned a pair of talented graphic artists to produce a series of drawings showing all the members of the production team – including himself – in various tragic positions. Some were taking poison, some leaping from bridges, some stabbing themselves and, finally, Bunce the editor was hanging from a gallows.

To accompany this apology Michael played over the final credits a record of a very tragic pop-song called 'I apologize': 'If I told a lie, if I made you cry, then I'm sorry ...' It went on, and on, and on. By the end of the song and the procession of little drawings, not only had the apology for a 'lie' been more than fully given, I would have thought that Isaac Woolfson was beginning to regret ever having asked for it in the first place.

Therefore, perhaps, the rule about lying on television should read: 'If you get caught telling a lie – apologize in style.'

There is an exception. You can tell a lie quite deliberately on television, if you can claim that it's a joke – and was always intended to be one. The only way to prove your intention beyond argument is to make it an April Fool joke. There have been many classic April Fool jokes on television but those who try it have to be more careful than their colleagues in newspapers and magazines. It is too easy to succeed, be taken seriously – and start the kind of panic that the first radio broadcast in America of H. G. Wells' 'War of the Worlds' produced, when people listening really did think that

Orson Welles was telling them that the Martians had landed.

The classic BBC April Fool joke is the one that was used on 'Panorama' by Richard Dimbleby. It almost certainly worked as effectively as it did because Richard Dimbleby and 'Panorama' were not only part of the establishment, they practically *were* the establishment. It was unthinkable that irreverence like a practical joke should come from so sombre a source. But it did.

Richard, in the studio, talked of disaster threatening farmers in Northern Italy. 'We've just brought back a film report from there,' he said. The film showed rows of devastated spaghetti trees. Hanging from the branches were strings of limp spaghetti. Ruined, Dimbleby explained, by early frosts which had taken all the starch and stiffness out of a harvest on which so many Italians relied for a living. He spoke of the potential unemployment and personal misery that the failure of the spaghetti harvest was likely to cause.

Back in the studio he signed off that Monday night's edition of 'Panorama' and said 'goodnight'. Millions of viewers, like us, had been completely taken in. It was hours before it dawned on me, for one, that spaghetti doesn't grow on trees.

The effect on the nation was as if a favourite Aunt had said 'Screw it'. Shock mingled with delight.

It was reported in *The Times*. The joke had, in itself, become an event.

By the time Esther and 'That's Life!' decided they could produce a practical joke the viewing public was far less reverential about BBC programmes and more suspicious of what they saw on their screens. Therefore, the 'lie' had to be utterly convincing.

For months film directors and reporters had been filming pets whose proud owners had nominated them for some outstanding talent – a show-jumping hamster, a housewife dog. Pets are hell to film – the directors had had them to the eyeballs. What better subject for a 'send up'.

They went out to film the story of an Old English Sheepdog who had been taught by his owner to drive a car.

The risks were appalling. Director Nick Handel is six foot four inches tall, reporter Chris Serle is six foot six inches tall. Together with a sound man and a cameraman they all managed to get into the back of the mini estate – a feat worthy of the *Guinness Book of Records* on its own.

The Old English Sheepdog, looking more like the Dulux dog than the advert, dragged his owner out of the house and climbed into the car. The pedals of the car had been extended so that the dog's feet could reach them. At least gear changes weren't necessary because it was an automatic, and the dog steered with one paw on each side of the central spoke in the steering wheel. They confined the dog's driving expedition to quiet suburban streets, still shocking a few pedestrians, some walking their own dogs. Suddenly a motorcycle traffic policeman overtook them, stopped them and, clearly unable to believe his eyes, asked the owner if the dog had passed its test.

The dog accelerated away leaving the policeman standing in rage at the roadside. The owner said conversationally to Chris Serle: 'I'm not too bothered – after all, who'll believe that copper's story when he gets back to the station?' By then we thought the audience might have worked out the date – April the first. Actually very few did.

How was it done? There was, of course, a real Old English Sheepdog, and a mini, with extended pedals. But there was also a marvellous lady variety artist who specializes in performing dressed up in an Old English Sheepdog costume. She was hired surreptitiously, briefed in obscure cutting rooms – she never even came to the office, in case the joke was blown too soon.

So, with brilliant film direction, the viewers saw the real sheepdog get into the car, and even glance back at the camera from the driver's window. But they didn't realize that all the relevant driving shots actually had the lady performer in the driving seat, with her feet on the pedals and hands on the steering wheel – in her shaggy sheepdog 'skin' made of curly nylon.

Unfortunately the April Fool joke rebounded on us. Because it was so convincing most of the viewers believed what they'd seen. BBC switchboards were jammed with complaints about the irresponsible attitude of the programme. But, eventually, the *Daily Express* revealed the truth and the film has since been re-shown a number of times as a classic April Fool joke. But we still meet viewers, not necessarily gullible or simple, who scold us indignantly for allowing a dog to drive a car – and, worse, allowing the dog to drive off after being stopped by a policeman.

People who complain seriously that the television camera lies about their opinions or arguments are often, in fact, complaining about the effect created by editing, either videotape or film editing. 'I spoke for nearly an hour and you only showed a couple of minutes' is quite a common complaint.

It's odd that they mind much less when they are edited for a newspaper article. Even the most distinguished politician finds it quite acceptable to give an interview to a newspaper reporter for an hour or more and then see only three or four hundreds words in print. That will produce no complaint from the politician, or anybody else for that matter. Any reservations they may have are likely to be concerned with the accuracy of the reporter's work and the faithfulness with which the interviewee's opinions have been reported, not the length of the article.

It's a pity, therefore, that the same clear understanding never appears to apply to television. Perhaps it's because it is a more dramatic medium to which people react emotionally rather than with clear heads. Few current affairs programmes will actually shoot an interview at a greater ratio than ten times the final length and most of them will keep to an even lower ratio than that. The reason is not just journalistic discipline but the fact that the cost of film alone has now reached the horrifying figure of ten pounds a minute – and is still rising.

And yet, perhaps, it is understandable that ten minutes in front of a film camera – let alone sixty minutes – makes even experienced speakers feel as if they have been treated grandly and, therefore, they become more sensitive to editing. But there is one way to ensure that your answers are used in a television programme as completely as you would wish. Harold Wilson learned it long ago.

Number your points. 'In reply to that question, David/ Robert/Alistair/Desmond, I would like to say five things . . .' And the interviewer's heart sinks to his boots. He will recognize a masterly move on the chess board. He knows his fate when he hears his interviewee continue: 'Point one . . .'; followed by 'Point two . . .'; followed by 'Point three . . .' and so on. If the interviewee is a truly old hand – and viewers should remember that most public figures, such as leading politicians, log up far more airtime than their interviewer – then the interviewee will raise his hand, in vision, close to his face, so that even the tightest picture framing won't cut it out, and then tick off the numbered points on his fingers. No one can drop a single point without the viewers noticing – the politician has it all his own way.

It's a trick which seldom fails. But a word of caution to any politicians who may be making a mental note to use it themselves. The alternative is to cut the interview altogether. Film editors have a phrase for that too, as they throw such material into the waste bin: 'Bye-Bye, clever clogs.'

In reality, television has to be a much more faithful way of reproducing what you really say, than newspaper journalism is. A newspaper reporter can mishear what you're saying and print a 'yes' for a 'no' – the unscrupulous reporters can even put words into your mouth, words that you would never dream of saying. But a camera and a microphone record actual words and real events, making it very hard to be mistaken about what is happening or being said.

Once, we came face to face with the problem of trying to film a very 'creative' newspaper story. When Esther was working on 'Braden's Week' they read a story in a local paper about a Phantom Gnome Nobbler. It was a dramatic tale. Garden gnomes and elves and little fishermen were, it seemed, being knocked off at an alarming rate by somebody who obviously had a grudge against them. The Phantom Gnome Nobbler had struck Folkestone. It was clearly an important piece of investigative television. Esther and James Kenelm Clarke, the film director, rang the two journalists who had written the story and arranged to meet them in a pub in Folkestone.

The journalists seemed a little jumpy but the team put it down to camera nerves. They introduced Esther to a local gnome manufacturer and the team were amazed at how very like a gnome the man himself looked, with a round tummy and a cherry-red, turned up nose. The second interviewee was a local ambulance man who didn't have any direct connection with gnomes at all and very kindly ignored Esther's terrible puns when she asked him if it could be a political campaign – 'an anti-Vietgnome demonstration'.

But the third interviewee made the story stand up. She was a lady with more gnomes in her garden than most people have blades of grass. And she was now a lady in fear. She had become so alarmed by the story in her local newspaper that she put barbed wire round her garden. She even refused to be interviewed facing the camera, in case the Gnome Nobbler followed her home from the supermarket to nobble her gnomes.

Esther interviewed her with her back to camera and she even played 'Gnome sweet Gnome' for the 'Braden's Week' team on her Hammond organ.

It made a moving film, with many close-ups of barbed wire and cowering gnomes. It was only on the way home that the director realized that, apart from the two journalists who'd written the story for the local newspaper in the first place, no one else had mentioned any gnomes actually being nobbled. They hadn't seen any nobbled gnomes. They had no real evidence that it had ever happened.

It was far more likely that two bored journalists driving round Folkestone one afternoon had got so sick of garden gnomes that they'd invented the whole story – and then had to run round like flies trying to make it stand up, using kind friends as interviewees when the television film cameras arrived. The lady with the barbed wire was clearly genuine but what she had been frightened by was not actually a gnome nobbler but an imaginary gnome nobbling invention.

They used the story in the programme and in the studio Esther went mad. The word gnome lends itself to punning almost better than any other. She was finally threatened with violence by Bernard Braden, if she didn't shut up, but not before she'd already suggested that the nobbler could be a 'gnomosexual' or that 'a gnome by any other gnome would smell as sweet' or that it ought to be a matter for the 'Gnome Office' to investigate and 'gnome is where the heart is' and 'a gnome of your own' . . . and more, and more.

12 Glittering prizes – and awful boobs

Awards nights are the culmination, the public reward and recognition by one's fellow professionals, of the work we do in television. The presentation of the awards is usually seen by the viewer – often at great, indulgent length – on the screen itself. But the occasion is really the profession talking to itself.

It's no bad thing that, once a year at least, directors, producers, and performers should find themselves judged for their work and rewarded for their talents. Awards nights are, however, occasions with a special spirit and atmosphere of their own, more closely related to the red blooded jealousies and vanities of Hollywood and the Oscars ceremony.

At the British Academy Awards smiles are never removed – and knives are barely concealed. ITV and BBC, defector and newcomer, mingle in social harmony, or so they all pretend. Everybody turns up, from director-generals to assistant film editors. Not to go is a dangerous gesture. It will be judged as arrogance – or cowardice. You are likely to be assassinated in your absence. Traditionally at such events the junior members of our profession can get a little drunk and insult the most senior – but not the other way round.

The food is usually awful and the awards and prizes for the most important jobs in the industry – as far as the industry itself is concerned – are invariably considered not glamorous enough for the viewers by the producers of the television broadcast and are handed out during the commercial breaks.

The evening goes on, it seems, for ever; an interminable procession of freshly shaved and bathed producers and performers receiving the Royal handshake, the bronze mask and being allowed the 'I couldn't have done it if it hadn't been for everybody else' twelve-second speech.

Anyway, every so often Morecambe and Wise will put on a little act, Charles Aznavour will sing a soulful ballad, or Pan's People will leap about on the stage. For those actually present at the awards the illusion of entertainment can be somewhat spoiled by having three heavily perspiring ladies from Pan's People crouched under your tablecloth ready to spring into muscular action from a surprise position, as far as the viewers are concerned. On the year that happened to my table I rather cheekily offered one of the dancers a drink under the tablecloth and she nearly missed her cue.

But if you're asked to attend because it's just possible you may receive an award you daren't say 'no'. And if you're one of the half dozen people in the country asked to host the occasion, or co-host it, you would certainly limp from a sick bed rather than miss the event.

It is, after all, the Number One occasion of our own profession – perhaps indulgent as far as the viewers are concerned but vital for us. When Esther was asked to co-host the British Academy Awards with Roger Moore she said 'yes'. I think she would have said yes if she'd been asked to the opening of a parking meter in Wigan with Roger Moore. The awards were due to be presented by the patron of the British Academy of Film and Television Arts, Princess Anne.

In order to broadcast an occasion like an awards night the presenters are invariably equipped with radio microphones. This involves a small microphone pinned to the front of a dress or a shirt and a transmitter the size of a cigarette pack concealed somewhere under your clothes, usually in the small of the back, to allow room for three feet of flexible wireless aerial to hang down. On a man this system is easy. The microphone goes on to the lapel, the transmitter in his hip pocket. For a woman the microphone usually goes somewhere convenient on the front of her dress and the transmitter is in the small of her back on a length of elastic round her waist. All performers have learned to switch off their transmitters before making nervous last-minute visits to the loo – otherwise you're likely to transmit every intimate moment to the studio audience waiting for the show to start.

Esther's problem was a faulty radio microphone. There were only minutes to go before the programme was due on the air. An embarrassed and charming sound assistant needed to change her transmitter and replace it with a good one. The transmitter was underneath her long dress, strapped in the small of her back. There was nothing else for it. Up came the glittery, spangled evening dress over her head, while the sound assistant started to untie the transmitter.

At that moment Princess Anne walked into the backstage area to reassure everybody and have a chat before the show started. Roger Moore proved, once again, why he was entirely the right man to play James Bond. Having shaken hands with Princess Anne and Captain Mark Phillips, he turned to the shape alongside him – an inside-out spangled evening dress in a large bundle, with a pair of Marks and Spencer's knickers and tights beneath – and a man on his knees behind it. 'You've met Esther Rantzen before haven't you ma'am?' he asked. 'She's the lady whose smile everybody recognizes.'

The broadcast that night was particularly effective. The warm relationship between Esther and Roger was quite noticeable and helped give the awards ceremony a special lift. Princess Anne even seemed more than usually relaxed. It was only after the programme that I learned why.

Awful moments, the kind that you spend the rest of your life trying to forget, the acute embarrassment, the terrible *faux pas*, the accidental insult, occur in the lives of everybody. But for those who appear on television the awful boob becomes part of television's history – with their names attached as author.

I still wake up shivering when I remember suggesting to an interviewee that his answer had been 'a tangenital one'. And I am forever grateful to Frank Cousins, the great trade union leader, who didn't blink when I suggested to him that his membership, the Transport and General Workers Union, might feel he had 'misled' them – I pronounced it to rhyme with 'bristled'. I'd only ever read the word before, I'd never heard it pronounced.

Sporting commentators live with danger – like tight-rope walkers, inevitably destined to fall off. Frank Bough remembers a colleague at the 1972 Munich Olympic games when the British kayak team were doing their best in the white water section to keep the flag – and themselves – up. Their best wasn't proving to be as good as the efforts produced by other countries. On the television screen it could be seen that they were upside down in a roaring torrent, trapped against a rock, clearly unable to right themselves. Equally clearly they were drowning. There was one of those long moments without commentary as perhaps a hundred million viewers around the world studied their television screens with interest and anticipation. Then the BBC commentator managed to do his stuff. With bright jingoistic enthusiasm he said: 'It looks as if our chances of the gold are slipping a little . . .'

Another classic boob has now gone down in television history as the result of the newly discovered passion for snooker among viewers. At a critical moment in one game the commentator described the position of the next ball that needed to be 'potted'. Then he added, 'and for those of you watching in black and white it's just behind the blue . . .'

Esther once interviewed Dennis Wheatley and the interview became a boob. She was fascinated to meet the author of so many best-selling books and she spent many hours researching a careful list of questions, designed to bring out the best in this distinguished man. Before the first question the programme showed a clip from a film based on one of his books. To Esther's horror Dennis Wheatley fell fast asleep. He was still asleep when the film ended and he continued to sleep as she asked her first question. She took a deep breath and kicked him. Dennis Wheatley opened his eyes and started to speak – what's more it was almost an answer to the question.

Huw Wheldon, on the other hand, once enthusiastically confronted and dealt with a dilemma live on the air. During an edition of the arts programme 'Monitor' he spoke the introduction to a piece of film. The film failed to arrive on the screen. It is one of the worst moments in any presenter's life. What do you do? Play the guitar? Sing? Waffle?

Huw Wheldon was an old hand, with nerves of steel, not easily thrown. He tried again. Somewhat stern-jawed when the film failed to appear for the second time he explained to the viewers that there was some technical trouble and that he hoped by now it would be sorted out. He reminded them of his introduction once more. Still nothing.

No film, no explanation, no telephone ringing, no piece of paper handed in from the side. Huw Wheldon displayed his mettle: 'You'd think forty highly-paid technicians could manage to roll one small piece of film between them, wouldn't you?' he exploded to camera. At that instant the film appeared on the screen. History doesn't record, and Huw Wheldon won't confess, what some of the 'highly-paid technicians' said to him after the programme.

As you may have spotted, it is nearly always dreadful machines that produce the most humiliating boobs. There's even a technical phrase for it in television – 'Sod's Law'. It means the film runs out just as President Jimmy Carter is announcing his decision to run for a second term, or Prime Minister Margaret Thatcher has started a sentence with the words 'Well, truthfully speaking, I think I must do a U-turn on this . . .' or the winning goal is about to be booted home. 'Sod's Law' also has human variations.

I once spent seventy-two hours continuously filming, without sleep, the lightning evangelical visit of an American 'hot gospel' preacher to this country. His speciality was reducing audiences of thousands of teenagers to crescendos of sobbing confessions. Weeping young men and women would crowd round him as he forgave them – and won them to the cause. His methods were viewed with considerable doubt by the religious establishment of this country and his converts were viewed with equal astonishment by their parents and relatives when they arrived home in a tear-stained state. It was a natural investigation for 'Man Alive' and we decided to film every minute of the preacher's visit to this country and then do a follow up to see how effective and durable some of his conversions were.

The climax of the preacher's evangelical tour was a giant meeting in Bristol. More than two thousand teenagers queued, sobbing, to be embraced by the preacher – and forgiven by God. As far as we can tell, it was the two thousandth and first who stole every box of recording tape we had left in the wings of the stage; tape containing all the material we had shot up until that moment.

The language used by our sound recordist and cameraman, and echoed by director Michael Latham, was hardly a fitting accompaniment to a religious tour. In a break in the proceedings I told the evangelist what had happened. Immediately he took it upon himself to recruit God, and his new converts, to recover our tapes. He made an impassioned appeal from the platform.

'It may be,' he said, 'that whoever took this magnetic tape belonging to the great, sincere, British Broadcasting Corporation would rather his heart was only inspected by God – and his deeds should not be visible to his fellow man.

'So everybody here – all two thousand of us – will close our eyes and pray for the person who did this. We will love the person who did this. We will stretch out our hearts to the person who did this – but we will do it secretly with our eyes closed. While our eyes are shut, and we promise that person in the name of Our Lord our eyes will stay shut, nobody will see that person put back the boxes of magnetic tape.

Now we will shut our eyes and pray for two minutes.' And we all did.

I must confess that I peeped. If I saw the bastard I was going to let him put back the tapes and then I was going to kill him. Maybe God knew what was in my heart and told the thief. I think I am the only person who did open his eyes. Michael Latham claimed that he was praying even harder than the Evangelist and his eyes were even tighter shut. But that night was the Devil's night. The tape wasn't returned and we had to put out our 'Man Alive' film 'Jesus Wept' using only half the material we'd shot. It was still a good film, but I've often wondered which sobbing worshipper went home clutching enough reels of magnetic tape to keep his hi-fi system operating for a century or more.

'Sod's Law' also applies to nature. It is one of nature's laws – and is probably why the apple fell on Newton's head rather than at his feet. I met 'Sod's Law' in one of its more dramatic natural forms at twenty degrees below zero while wearing my thermal underwear. We were high in the Wyoming mountains, at Jackson Hole, filming one of the 'Americans' documentaries on the life of a rancher, in the middle of winter.

I was due to make a statement to camera explaining the hardships of a rancher's life, during winter in the Rockies. The country was deep in snow and all of us were wearing inner felt boots, insulated moonboots outside and many layers of insulated clothing. The panorama behind the spot chosen for me to stand was devastating. Miles of virgin snow stretched into the distance to join the forests and the peaks of the Teton range of mountains, the same range against which they shot my favourite cowboy film, *Shane*. Nat Crosby, the cameraman, insisted that I should do my piece to camera in one take, no fluffs, no mistakes. Then I could turn away from camera and walk into the distance across the virgin snow. It was to be a shot which would go down in film history, he assured the young director, Tristan Allsop, and me.

Crouched shivering under a pine tree, Tristan and I rehearsed and rehearsed until we were both sure I was word perfect with the thirty-second piece to camera. There could be no second attempt. It might be four months before another snow fall produced the same virgin background.

I took up my position. Nat Crosby studied the sun, the temperature of his frozen camera and pronounced himself satisfied. 'Action,' said Tristan. I spoke my lines, I remembered them, I didn't fluff, I didn't make a mistake. Overjoyed at the end of the little piece I smiled at the camera and turned to make my 'exit' walking towards the distant mountains across the virgin snow. I promptly vanished to shoulder level in the deepest drift I've ever encountered.

Terrified of stopping, throbbing with the knowledge that there were no second chances, I continued to walk. I sank deeper and deeper. Later Tristan told me that all that could be seen clearly was the bobble on my little woolly hat sticking above the snow, with puffs of steam coming out as I muttered curses like a Marine.

Needless to say we filmed it again, the next day, in another location and my heroic efforts were never broadcast. They did make another moment at the film editor's Christmas party, though.

But in the end the machines will win. The best we'll ever be able to do, while we wait for that day, is to talk of the times we've survived the threat of technology. Esther is determined to avoid such a moment at all costs. And does so with admirable skill.

Her series 'The Big Time' was invented by her entirely as a defence against the machines. Bryan Cowgill, who was the Controller of BBC-1, had decided to use Esther in another kind of programme as well as 'That's Life!' He wanted a series of films called 'Fly Me to the Moon' in which Esther was to be used as a guinea-pig to try out hair-raising jobs. The first job he had in mind was to have her trained as a lady astronaut and launched into space, preferably on a trip to the moon. What's more he was quite serious.

When I'd finished spluttering he was still serious. 'You can fix it, Desmond,' he told me. 'If anybody can fix it you can. And if anybody can do it she can.'

I took the idea home. It met with the kind of reception I had expected. Zero. 'It could work,' I told her. 'It won't hurt a lot and you'd be very good at it and it needn't be dangerous and, in a different way George Plimpton has already done it in America with sporting things and training as a comedian to appear in Las Vegas.' She was adamant – and terrified. And there is nothing so adamant as the terrified. 'I'd love to produce, or report, a series in which other people were given the opportunity, as amateurs, to test their skills in highly exciting professional fields,' she said. 'Such as a trapeze artist in the circus, or conducting a symphony orchestra, or riding the winning horse in a steeplechase.' And so 'The Big Time' was born.

When I went back to Bryan Cowgill, rather fearfully confessing that I had been unable to persuade his consumer producer/presenter to fly to the moon (she was my wife, too) he was unsurprised. 'I knew that would push you two into coming up with something good,' he told me. He has always held the view, it turned out, that the most inventive thinking comes from people invited to consider the sacrifice of others as an alternative to their own martyrdom.

13 The organization – and top people

You can always tell how important a television executive is by the number of initials after his name – Bill Cotton is now DMDTel. for instance – the Deputy Managing Director of BBC Television. The ultimate of course is the Director-General who is actually addressed by his initials. 'Good morning, DG', 'Have some coffee, DG'. They even have a senior executive whose job is to make sure that when a BBC man is promoted the initials of his new job don't spell something rude or funny. But he must have been out to lunch when a friend of ours was promoted to be in charge of magazine programmes in radio and designated Head of CAMP (Current Affairs Magazines Programmes).

At least there are people in the BBC who still find the 'letters after your name' game a source of great amusement – even if they can't stop it happening. Two members of the BBC news staff once decided to prove their worst fears about the BBC as an organization – and succeeded beyond their wildest dreams.

They discovered an empty office at the Television Centre and started writing memos, directed all round the Corporation, from that office demanding information on the off duty patterns, habits and hobbies of staff in other departments. They enquired about preferences for holidays, inclinations for winter sports, whether staff would like to split their holidays and so on. The signature on the bottom of the memo was invariably illegible but the BBC title at the top was quite clear: Head of Leisure Services – HOLS.

It should have been spotted immediately. The BBC departmental heads should have noticed that somebody was 'sending them up'. Instead, the replies started to come in thick and fast – to the empty office. The two members of the news staff, whiling away the long night shifts, sent out more enquiries. How many husbands and wives took separate holidays? How many members of the BBC staff would like more BBC organized leisure activity, on BBC premises?

It could have gone on for ever. But the BBC accounts department, to whom one of the memos about leisure services had been copied, grew anxious. They realized they had not been told about a new appointment, Head of Leisure Services, they worried that they weren't paying him at the proper grade and with the proper allowances. Accountants are conscientious people, so a member of the accounts department was sent to explain to this new Head of Department why he wasn't being paid and to ensure that the matter was put right at once. The whole deceit was discovered. The empty office and the two men of the news staff were caught in the act. They were reported and disciplined for misusing BBC equipment and supplies – paper and typewriters. In our opinion they should have been given a bonus, even a mention in the honours list. But 'de-bunking' isn't often recognized as a major art.

Professionally it's actually impossible to avoid initials. They've become the jargon of the trade. In the control rooms of studios round the world it has become the only way, quickly and simply, to cue into action the machinery, and the people, of television. I've often wondered if all those bachelor viewers who used to wait so lasciviously for Anna Ford to appear with the 'News at Ten' would have felt the same about her if they knew that she only arrived on the screen via a series of incomprehensible shouts and commands. 'Stand by TK45, coming to you VT7, zoom into Big Ben, fade up sound, stand by studio, cue Anna, cut to three.' And all of that just to get you away from the picture of Big Ben ...

Both of us actually admire people who push back at organizations. After all, 'That's Life!' and 'Man Alive' would never have been invented if we didn't. Although it doesn't do to say so too often, an organization like the BBC needs pushing back at from time to time. And they know it. It keeps it healthy and in good spirits.

The BBC occupies many buildings, quite a few of them round Shepherd's Bush. One impressive gloomy looking warehouse is the old Gainsborough studios in Lime Grove. Over the years that top BBC programmes like Panorama and Nationwide have been broadcast from Lime Grove there have been an impressive collection of top names trapped when the antiquated lift has jammed between floors. I once spent an hour imprisoned in it with Harold Wilson, during which time we both knew the programme he'd arrived to appear in had finished. He was very good about it and not anything like as claustrophobic and twitchy as I became.

Over the years, too, Lime Grove has grown, and gradually the terraced houses adjoining the old film studios have been bought by the BBC and converted into production offices. Except one house. Beautifully and stubbornly maintained with roses in the front garden, it belonged, we were told, to a Polish family who for years persistently resisted every blandishment and persuasion the BBC could offer. Even when the BBC owned all the houses on both sides this family refused to sell. As a result, getting from one production office to another in the BBC 'houses' in Lime Grove frequently involves a detour into the open air (and the rain) around the back of the privately owned dissenter in the ranks of Lime Grove. It annoys the architects, infuriates the maintenance men and is uncomfortable for the staff.

But Esther and I, and quite a few BBC executives, always mentally tip our hats with pleasure whenever we pass that one house. After all, in the BBC we should be the first to recognize and admire the British bulldog spirit – even if it is a Polish family that's showing us how to do it.

It was at Lime Grove that Esther was forced by the organization to become a forger. There is only a small car park there, reserved mainly for bosses, and no parking places for the likes of workers. People with access to parking spaces in the BBC have a pass in the windscreen of their car which, in those days, consisted of a white circle with a red triangle in it and the letter C stamped on the centre. (In the status game a good car park pass is more important than office curtains). Esther was determined to put an end to a life of misery in which she spent hours between cutting rooms, studios and Lime Grove, driving around looking for a parking space three or four times a day – and usually winding up with a parking ticket, invariably with a jokey 'Ah well, That's Life!' scrawled on it. I should have realized that she was up to no good when she vanished into the front garden one day with a pad and a couple of felt pens 'to do a sketch for the replanting of the front bed'. She was actually making a very credible imitation of my car park pass which she then stuck in the windscreen of her mini.

She says now that she didn't tell me because she didn't want to compromise my integrity. It was weeks before I discovered what had happened. And in the meantime she parked happily among the bosses at Lime Grove until a sharp-eyed ex-marine security man spotted the forgery and reported it. But before she could be formally expelled a letter arrived in 'That's Life!' from a con man who had been investigated by the team. It was an angry letter quite specific about what was going to happen to Esther Rantzen. He said he'd punch all her teeth down her throat – and he knew exactly where she worked, what time she arrived, and left, which door she came through. He'd be waiting. The organization came out in its true colours. Esther Rantzen must be protected from possible injury. She must be allowed to drive through the barriers into the car park so that she need not be at risk. She was immediately issued with the correct car park pass.

And the man in charge scribbled a note at the bottom of his protective memo: 'You'll probably find this one works nearly as well as the forgery we've been admiring for weeks.'

The organization depends on men in uniforms. And what the men in uniform most respect is another uniform. When Emily was only three months old Esther was asked by the BBC to start working again on 'That's Life!' This meant the baby had to be brought in to her at lunchtime so that they could both see each other – and have lunch. Our nanny, Lizzie, was a devoted and conscientious girl who looked great in jeans and a sweatshirt, the ideal gear for handling damp babies. But whenever she arrived at the BBC, swinging the Moses basket, the arm of officialdom would stop her. Uniforms, we discovered, were the answer. Much to her rage Lizzie had to start coming to work at lunchtime in the smart blue nanny's uniform which we admired greatly – and she hated. It worked like a charm.

'The Cook has one, but we never watch it,' used to be the pretence of all those Top People. Actually they usually did have one, hidden away in the study, but never in the sitting room. These days only Malcolm Muggeridge boasts about not having one – and doesn't let it stop him earning a lot of money from appearing on it. He talks of having had his aerial taken out and says it didn't hurt a bit. Nowadays top people watch the telly. More to the point, they try very hard to influence the telly.

The 'top person's' phone call after a programme goes straight to the Director-General or the Managing Director now. 'Our video recorder broke down last night, while we were at the opera, and I understand that dreadful current affairs programme of yours got it all wrong again so perhaps you wouldn't mind popping a transcript in a taxi straight away and I'll get back to you when I've worked out the kind of apology that will do.'

Pressure like this on the Old Boy Network is resisted. Unfortunately, not always successfully. The most influential members of the establishment, those who once regarded it as a kind of electric comic for the domestic staff, have woken up to its full potency. And they would like to limit and control its choice of targets.

Cabinet ministers almost always demand the last word in any debate. They reject the thought that such pressure is far from democratic. They're in the game to win. Politicians, doughty and battle-scarred with decades of parliamentary debate behind them, fight to be elected at the hustings, often coping with abuse, the shriek of the heckler and the occasional cry of a voter with awkward questions demanding answers.

But if you wish to bring those same politicians into a studio with ordinary members of the public, then they complain – at the highest level. Ask them to join in debate with the homeless, or the jobless – or even worse, the feckless – and you will see them reaching, like frightened maidens caught in the bathroom, for the covering dignity of parliamentary pomposity.

Very few institutions, or even significant social groups in our society, ever feel they have been properly represented on television. Trade unionists feel that their activities are only reported, and then aggressively, when they are on strike. The fact that good news is no news rightly irritates their sense of fair play. Industrialists and leading businessmen feel, equally strongly, that the perils of the boardroom and the grind of successfully running a large business organization are too often shown on television in caricature and parody.

But the professional institutions are among the most paranoiac. The medical profession vies with the law for top place in that league. Doctors and surgeons, particularly, sometimes behave as though television should never be allowed to discuss medicine, or patients, or pain. Certainly not with the patients. Doctor knows best. Lawyers behave with the same kind of paranoia. Architects use their professional status to shield themselves from journalistic inquiries. Accountants don't like being asked publicly to account for themselves. Quantity surveyors, on the other hand, have recently been complaining of too little exposure on television.

But top people can be stimulating because the acquisition of power, authority, wealth or responsibility makes them behave differently. (The 'difference' is the interesting thing.) When I had lunch with Sir Robert Mark in order to discuss the one hour face-to-face interview he had agreed to give me, on his retirement, he arrived wearing a gun in a shoulder holster. I suggested to him that there weren't too many potential assassins in the Arts Club and that in any case I was nervous that he might make a mistake and shoot my toe off. But Robert Mark is an excellent shot and not unaware of his potential as a 'target' for lunatics or terrorists. I do remember that the producer of that programme – already a man with a reputation for nervousness – became almost speechless every time Sir Robert leaned forward across the lunch table and the producer could gaze into his jacket. It had on him the sort of effect that Marilyn Monroe's cleavage might well have had on others.

My old boss, Sir Hugh Cudlip, when he agreed to be the subject of a filmed profile 'Publish and Be Damned', became so enthusiastic about the project that it was difficult to stop him directing the camera personally. We even began referring to him, privately, as 'Cecil-B-de-Cudlip'. He planned extensive, and expensive, locations for us in order, he said, to jazz up his own visual image. He included a trip on his motor yacht on the Solent and received no objections from me as I've always been a willing volunteer to haul on ropes and fall off other people's boats.

But Hugh Cudlip was not for nothing the Chairman of the Daily Mirror Group and the man who led the tabloid revolution of the 50s. He agreed to be interviewed only at the wheel of his yacht. This meant quite a crowd squeezed into the wheelhouse. Hugh Cudlip at the helm, the cameraman, the soundman, me to ask the questions, the director – and Hugh's parrot. This last participant was sprung upon us just as we entered the swell at the mouth of the Hamble river. 'The parrot goes everywhere with me,' announced Hugh, 'and it wouldn't seem right to my friends if he wasn't on my shoulder while I was speaking to you. I've had another idea.' I heard the director, Harry Weisbloom, stifle a groan behind me. 'We'll open this interview with me on the radio telephone to the *Daily Mirror* asking them how it's going and what news has been breaking.' We knew there was no point in arguing.

Squeezed together, swaying from side to side, listening to the soundman's stomach grumble as he turned green, we prepared for the interview. Sir Hugh Cudlip, one hand on the wheel, parrot on his shoulder, reached for the hand-set of the ship-to-shore telephone. We slopped about in the wake of a huge container ship that had just bulldozed down Southampton Water in front of us. Sir Hugh placed the phone to his ear and started to bellow at a totally perplexed *Daily Mirror* newsroom, well used to many of his eccentricities but still alarmed to find their boss ringing them up from sea demanding to know what was in the paper 'because the parrot was getting restless, and the film crew were looking seasick'.

At this point the parrot bit Hugh Cudlip on the ear – hard. There then followed a string of language, familiar to me from the old days and comforting to the puzzled executives at the *Daily Mirror*. Thank God, at last, they were hearing the voice and tones of the man they knew. I suppose I felt comforted too when the first words Hugh Cudlip uttered on that piece of film were, 'I'll sue the fucking BBC for that ...'

It isn't only the top people, although it's mostly them, who've learned the latest methods of bringing pressure to bear on the telly. If it weren't for that marvellous judge The Master of the Rolls, Lord Denning, who has such an acute understanding of truth and people, many a television programme would never have reached the air for the viewers. His Hampshire accent became the voice of sanity and common sense in our lives on a number of occasions when people were trying to stop us broadcasting. Lord Denning, thank heavens, watched and understood television, knew what programmes like 'That's Life!' and 'Man Alive' were trying to do and recognized some of the attempts to stifle us by using 'gagging writs' or injunctions.

Before Lord Denning came on the scene many injunctions to restrain us from broadcasting had succeeded. It was he who ruled consistently that a person had no right to restrict free speech. He knew that if we'd got it wrong we'd have to pay for it with libel damages, but he ruled that we shouldn't be restrained from an attempt to get it right just because certain people were frightened of what we might say about them.

After a while the kind of people who had reached for injunctions, frequently on an *ex parte* basis (applying to a judge without letting the other side know in advance of the application) started to reach for another device; the 'gagging' injunction. They would 'discover' (sometimes we suspected they would even initiate) some other legal action, perhaps a customer sueing them. They would then ask the court to rule that we should not broadcast because to do so would be a contempt of other court proceedings. Lord Denning consistently defended our right to broadcast.

There was also one occasion, which I remember vividly, when Esther's team investigated the conditions in which dogs and puppies were kept in a kennel in the Home Counties before being sold through a London pet shop. They found themselves faced with an injunction, granted on a Saturday to stop them broadcasting. Under normal circumstances the law, or its processes, may be slow, but on occasions such as this it moves with almost breathtaking speed. The BBC and 'That's Life!' appealed immediately. The appeal was heard in the dining room of the Kensington home of one of the Appeal Court judges at lunchtime on Sunday, only hours before 'That's Life!' was due to transmit. The knives and forks were pushed to one side as counsel, solicitors and clients for both sides argued their points in front of the judge. In the end, after nearly two hours of careful and courteous hearing in most unlegal surroundings, the BBC was given the right to go ahead with the programme.

As we left the elegant flat of the appeal judge I knew from the smell of burning Yorkshire pudding that we'd ruined his Sunday lunch. Not by a muscle had he betrayed any emotion of disquiet. In some countries we might have been shot.

Then, of course, there is the phone call from Downing Street. It happens more often than most viewers might imagine. I cannot remember a single occasion when the message was one of praise. Phrases like 'fair-minded', 'balanced', 'accurate' and 'justified' are never in my experience used in that kind of phone call.

But it would be a dull world if we were ignored – it's certainly a more interesting world when you read complaints about yourself in the papers even before you receive them. That's a political mechanism which has been practised by, among others, Mary Whitehouse. The BBC, quite rightly in our opinion, has taken to responding to such manoeuvres by answering press inquiries with the comment: 'When we receive the private letter, which appears to have been made public, then we will answer it – privately.' Very dignified too. But Mary Whitehouse doesn't mind sacrificing the odd piece of dignity in favour of a winning move or two for the campaign in which she passionately believes.

The problem about pressure – whether it be from Margaret Thatcher, Mary Whitehouse, the men in charge of a double glazing firm, or a complaining group of citizens – is not what it represents by way of complaint from outside the broadcasting organizations, but what it does to those inside. It is not the enemy without who is to be feared – but rather the fearful within. The real threat, for the viewers, is not censorship by the bosses but that programme makers may so fear the possibility of censorship that, in anticipation, they will step back from boldness or honest journalism.

14 The viewers

Nothing matters in our trade if they're not there. Nothing counts, nobody stays in business. Whatever goes on the screen, or behind it, has no meaning without the viewers. But sometimes you wouldn't think so.

Viewers are measured, counted, assessed, predicted, catered for and, just once in a while, heard from on the screen. But that last aspect is the most troublesome one and the thing that bothers the television bosses the most. Viewers tend to behave like people with minds of their own, sometimes refusing to be labelled and pigeonholed as programme makers and television executives would often like them to be.

One thing we have both learned is that the popular image many critics seem to have of the viewer sitting at home, brain addled and numb after hours of uncritical telly watching, is completely untrue. Viewers, in our experience, sit talking back to the programmes, sometimes even shouting at the screen. When their indignation boils over they express it with angry letters to the person who's provoked them.

Every time Esther splits an infinitive or wears a dress that's too daring, or if she makes a joke with a whisper of a double meaning, she gets letters dotted with exclamation marks and littered with many underlinings, usually in purple. The ruder the letter the more often it is anonymous. But, occasionally, angry viewers do attach their names and addresses and then Esther replies with a letter so mild, so charming – and so infuriatingly turning the other cheek – that it must double their apoplexy.

Of course, there are many other kinds of letters from viewers. Esther receives ten thousand a week and only half of them contain the saucy misquotes for Cyril Fletcher to read on the air. Many are deeply moving. When Esther took part in a programme about post-natal depression which, like many kinds of mental illness, had until then been a subject shrouded in silence and secrecy, she received a deluge of letters from women who had suffered, or the families of women who were suffering. Inspired by the viewers' letters she and the producer of the programme, together with *Woman* magazine, set up MAMA (The Meet-A-Mum Association), a national network of self-help support groups. The idea came from the viewers and has flourished because of the viewers. Now MAMA has an increasing membership with seventy different groups meeting regularly all over the country.

Viewers also help each other regularly via television programmes. 'That's Life!' once told the story of a man who had lost his job, his home, even his desire to live because of a series of catastrophes which began when he was conned by a pyramid-selling company and became trapped into a second mortgage and a pile of debt. The viewers saved him. As a result of the programme he was offered a job, which he still has to this day, and real encouragement and advice to get his life straight. His wife still knits woolly scarves for the 'That's Life!' researcher who investigated his story.

Occasionally friendships grow out of the letters we receive. Seven years ago a little girl and boy wrote a funny, cheeky letter to Esther, about 'That's Life!'. They came to the show and we've become firm friends. Now Clive, working for a living, and Pippa in her second year at Cambridge, are almost part of our family circle – not just viewers.

When Esther was telephoned by an extraordinarily brave

and bright young man who suffers from a muscular illness and is completely bedbound, she chatted to him out of interest at hearing from such a perceptive and critical viewer. That was more than five years ago. Now they talk to each other once a month and both of us find it rewarding to know that if he can't get out of his own room and explore the world himself, at least, through television, the world can come to him. He once told Esther that she was the only person, apart from his immediate family, who regularly talked to him. On the air she mentioned the idea of a 'phone friend' club for disabled people who might like to talk to each other. The idea took root and a splendid, energetic Scottish lady took on the task of organizing it.

But not all letters from viewers are complimentary. If you appear regularly enough on the television screen viewers sometimes come to believe you belong to them, because you've become familiar to them. Richard Baker constantly receives letters from viewers asking him to send them one of his ties. It's as though they feel he has an unlimited supply to give away. Esther receives at least fifteen letters a day asking her to donate something 'personal' for auction at a charity event. If she sent clothes she'd have nothing to wear. So, as both of us are compulsive readers of paperbacks, she usually autographs and sends off a book we've just finished.

Recently one viewer sent a book back to her with a brusque letter complaining that it wasn't very interesting, and could she kindly send something else. Mind you, in the same post she received a letter which read: 'Dear Miss Rantzen – Please investigate something nasty going on in the garages of South Croydon. I could write more about it, but my hand keeps shooting across the paper ...'

Sometimes the viewers fall in love. Not with us, but with their idea of us – an ideal that, sadly, we can't live up to. For years I received regular letters from a lady who used to draw a little sketch of herself with a water pitcher balanced on her head (a reference to some occasion she had once explained in one of her early twenty-page letters). She wrote sadly, sometimes irritably, in her unfulfilled passion. I found it particularly difficult when she wrote: 'I waited again last night under the clock at Victoria and you didn't show up – I know she forced you to stay at home.' There are no more letters from that lady viewer – nor have there been for some years now. I hope it's because she found somebody who did wait under the clock at Victoria Station, a real person, not an image on the screen.

Then there was the man who met Esther in the street while she was doing interviews. He not only fell for her, he became persistent, almost dangerous in his passion for her. He challenged me to a duel. Foolishly I took it for a joke and replied lightly. I should have known better. By return post he responded by demanding a place and a weapon. He went on to mention his service in the Guards and the parachute regiment where he had been a physical training instructor and had become an expert pistol shot and swordsman. In the same post he wrote to Esther telling her of the duel and assuring her 'I'll be round for you after it's over'. Luckily for me, according to his most recent letter, he is presently spending some time in one of Her Majesty's more secure establishments.

And there was the air mail letter from Libya written by a Nigerian to Esther: 'Hello Esther: Here comes the voice of someone you haven't meeten before in your life. But before I have something to say, I throw my love I have on you. I will first ask of your health and your condition living this time in Britain. I hope you are in good health as I am over here. Esther, I want to tell you of my feelings I have on you ...' At the top of the letter Mr George Armah, from a post office box in Bengazi, had also written 'You kiss before you read'. Touched at the gesture – but cautious nevertheless – Esther responded with two lines thanking him for his kind letter and good wishes. An avalanche of passion came back by return. More to the point, he revealed he was on his way to England, inspired, he said, by Esther's reply. Where should they meet? What arrangements would she like to make? This time she didn't have the nerve to reply.

The fact is it's clearly fun for viewers to be able to see

those famous screen faces in real life, to be able to compare the reality of blotchy flesh with Sun Goddess make-up. And that has led to a profitable industry for many television personalities – the personal appearance. Opening boutiques or baptizing petrol stations is an opportunity for the viewers to hire the telly people. And, of course, if a telly personality is invited to meet the viewers 'in the flesh' at a commercial occasion he or she will usually receive a pretty handsome fee.

The mayor of one town once invited Esther to open a new shopping precinct. Treading carefully, as consumer journalists must, she has never taken part in any of the highly profitable telly activities such as declaring a new supermarket open, or cutting the ribbon at a new shoe shop – just in case she may have to, in the next week or two, expose them as villains. But a whole shopping precinct sounded safe enough.

She arrived trying to look like a television personality. It's a mood I, personally, find endearing. She invariably borrows a hat from the 'Black and White Minstrel Show' and wears earrings that came out of a cracker – or at least look like it. Still, there she was, 'a telly personality meeting the viewers', apparently confident but actually underneath rather shy and nervous about occasions like this.

The first bad news was that the Mayor was an incorrigible 'toucher', the kind of man who'd crack a joke and instantly prod you in the ribs. He introduced Esther to all the dignitaries with his hot hand firmly round her waist. She got clammier and clammier.

Eventually they reached the shopping precinct and there she found rows of little display booths. Each one housed a grinning double-glazing salesman, a central-heating salesman, or a loft-conversion cowboy, all the villains she'd spent the last series of 'That's Life!' exposing.

This, it turned out, was their new patch, and they'd elected her to be the celebrity to shake hands with each one of them for the benefit of the photographers.

The Mayor didn't allow her a second to flinch or withdraw.

Round the carousel she went for the local newspaper photographers, the Mayor's hand getting stickier by the minute. At
every sales booth each con man smiled for the cameras,
shaking hands warmly with Esther – and afterwards tipped
her a triumphant wink. It was perfect revenge for them. She
was surprised to find out that con men avidly watch 'That's
Life!', cheering the villains and learning new tips.

But we do have other equally unexpected viewers.

Probably one of the most glamorous occasions we've ever
been to was the evening when Princess Anne opened the
cinema, which was named after her, in the British Academy
of Film and Television Arts Headquarters in Piccadilly.
Esther turned up for work that morning in what she cheerfully admits are rather bedraggled office clothes. We both
worked so late that evening that Esther had to change into her
smartest black chiffon in the back of the car.

She says, if you've never tried it, it's actually quite easy.
I would qualify that by pointing out that the only real
embarrassment is when a coach full of tourists pulls up
alongside you at traffic lights, and they all look down from the
coach windows at a pair of feet sticking out of the back
window of the car while the owner struggles into a clean
pair of tights. Nevertheless, we arrived at the Academy on
time, only mildly flushed with the exertions of changing
on the move.

When Princess Anne arrived to unveil the plaque dedi-
cating the theatre in her name she was accompanied by the
Queen and Prince Philip. The British Academy of Film and
Television Arts' elegant headquarters were only made possible in the first instance by a generous donation from the
Royal family, who had agreed that some of the profits from
the film *Royal Family* should go to the Academy to start them
off in a new home.

Princess Anne made an excellent speech to an audience
which consisted of a very small number of television personalities and programme makers, and a very large number of
bosses and television tycoons, who had also donated large

lumps of money to the Academy and for whom this evening was the reward.

The Queen, during Princess Anne's speech, spent most of the time looking around the audience with obvious interest. Neither of us realized quite how deeply interested the Queen is in the people who make television programmes.

When the speeches were over Esther and I went to the bar for a drink. Suddenly Esther started behaving as though she'd hit her thumb with a hammer, or someone was standing on the hem of the black chiffon. She had just realized that the young girl in the print frock with her back to us, only six inches away, was Princess Anne. She hissed at me:

'You never told me they were going to be in here, actually going to mingle.'

In fact, by now, both of us were finding it rather difficult to breathe as we found ourselves squashed tight in the centre of a group by the well upholstered hips, shoulders and behinds of the Director-General, the Managing Director of Television, the Managing Director of Radio and so many other bosses of the BBC that it felt as if all the oxygen was being extracted from the atmosphere. Mind you, we have both noticed that senior BBC management has that rather stifling effect.

Suddenly the clusters of grey-flannelled people around us begin to shift like ripples in a pond. It's not an effect we'd seen before and we looked to see what was causing the shifting and whispering. Coming towards us was one of the most familiar faces in the world. For a startling moment it was as if a pound note was walking straight at us. Or a stamp. It is extraordinary how much we all take for granted the fact that the Queen's face has become an everyday part of all our lives. And when it arrives in front of you in real life you stand there, rooted, paralysed.

Somebody introduced the Queen to all the bosses and she smiled at them. Then she turned to Esther and said:

'Did you get absolutely soaked last Sunday?'

For a moment Esther looked baffled and then she realized

that the Queen was referring to the previous week's 'That's Life!' when Esther had been drenched in soda water during some daft consumer test. Esther said she had, indeed, been soaked and the Queen went on:

'I do love all those marvellous old ladies you find in the street market.'

Esther mumbled an appreciative reply and the ranks of double-breasted tycoonery remained to attention, heads bent forward at a polite angle, smiles of apparent interest fixed on their faces but eyes gazing at Esther, unsmiling.

But the Queen was not ready to move on.

'Don't you find it very depressing unearthing so many swindles and confidence tricks?' she asked.

Esther told her the truth, which is that we have always found that the generosity and kindness of the viewers, when they respond to the story of someone who needs help, far outweighs the machinations of the con men and crooks we come across. We were both beginning to relax. Not only was it obvious that the Queen was an interested viewer, her questions revealed a very perceptive understanding of programmes. But the gentleman at her elbow finally moved her on and we were left in a little social vacuum. One television boss said icily to me:

'I suppose now Esther will want a gold plated microphone – or "By Royal Appointment" on the camera.'

My thoughts were interrupted when I was introduced to one of the Royal Ladies in Waiting. They are fascinating people, always discreetly in the background, like royal detectives – but invaluable. They do more than take over the royal bouquet or souvenir gift, more than just accompany the Queen or her family on official engagements. With diplomatic skill and experience they fill in behind the royal presence, make substantial what might otherwise be just a handshake and a fragment of a conversation. I have often met and admired Ladies in Waiting. I enjoyed chatting with this one about the occasion.

'You know I have a bone to pick with you people in television,' said the Lady in Waiting, with a smile. She explained that on their way there that evening the small royal convoy had been held up by traffic near Piccadilly. They had been worried that they might be late, and it is the Lady in Waiting's task to see that the Queen is always on time and never appears rushed or flustered.

'I tried to find out what was holding us up,' she said. 'Ahead of us there was a saloon car alongside a motor coach and, do you know, sticking out of the back window of the car were a woman's legs, wriggling. Right in the centre of all that traffic. In broad daylight. No wonder there was so much hooting and shouting from the charabanc. I don't know what London's coming to these days. I'm afraid I blame the television for it. Things have changed such a lot because of television.'

She was more accurate than she would ever know and I didn't have the nerve to tell her who owned the legs.

Anyway, who are we to question the opinion of any viewer? They are, each and every one of them, entitled to our affection, our loyalty and our gratitude. Where would we be without them? And what would our own lives be like if we ourselves couldn't be viewers too?

Index

Index

Selected Bestsellers

☐	**Gone with the Wind**	Margaret Mitchell	£2.95p
☐	**Robert Morley's Book of Worries**	Robert Morley	£1.50p
☐	**The Totem**	David Morrell	£1.25p
☐	**The Alternative Holiday Catalogue**	edited by Harriet Peacock	£1.95p
☐	**The Pan Book of Card Games**	Hubert Phillips	£1.50p
☐	**The New Small Garden**	C. E. Lucas Phillips	£2.50p
☐	**Food for All the Family**	Magnus Pyke	£1.50p
☐	**Everything Your Doctor Would Tell You If He Had the Time**	Claire Rayner	£4.95p
☐	**Rage of Angels**	Sidney Sheldon	£1.75p
☐	**A Town Like Alice**	Nevil Shute	£1.50p
☐	**Just Off for the Weekend**	John Slater	£2.50p
☐	**A Falcon Flies**	Wilbur Smith	£1.95p
☐	**The Deep Well at Noon**	Jessica Stirling	£1.75p
☐	**The Eighth Dwarf**	Ross Thomas	£1.25p
☐	**The Music Makers**	E. V. Thompson	£1.50p
☐	**The Third Wave**	Alvin Toffler	£1.95p
☐	**Auberon Waugh's Yearbook**	Auberon Waugh	£1.95p
☐	**The Flier's Handbook**		£4.95p

All these books are available at your local bookshop or newsagent, or can be ordered direct from the publisher. Indicate the number of copies required and fill in the form below

3

Name _____
(block letters please)

Address _____

_____

Send to Pan Books (CS Department), Cavaye Place, London SW10 9PG
Please enclose remittance to the value of the cover price plus:

25p for the first book plus 10p per copy for each additional book ordered to a maximum charge of £1.05 to cover postage and packing
Applicable only in the UK

While every effort is made to keep prices low, it is sometimes necessary to increase prices at short notice. Pan Books reserve the right to show on covers and charge new retail prices which may differ from those advertised in the text or eleswhere